CIM Companion:

marketing in practice

CIM Publishing

CIM Publishing

The Chartered Institute of Marketing
Moor Hall
Cookham
Berkshire
SL6 9QH

www.cim.co.uk

First published 2002
© CIM Publishing 2002

Series Editors: Mark Stuart and John Ling.

The publishers wish to acknowledge *People Management* magazine for its permission to include extracts from articles in this book.

British Library Cataloguing in Publication Data
A CIP catalogue record for this book can be obtained from the British Library.

ISBN 0 902130 95 1

Printed and bound by The Cromwell Press, Trowbridge, Wiltshire.
Cover design by Marie-Claire Bonhommet.

contents

Study guide

This Companion is written to complement the recommended core text by Dibb, Simkin, Pride and Ferrell, *Marketing Concepts and Strategies* (4th European Edition), published by Houghton Mifflin. It aims to offer you support as either an individual or group learner as you move along the road to becoming a competent and proficient marketer. This is a process of learning that has two important elements:

Understanding marketing concepts and their application

The following Sessions have been written to highlight the concepts that you will need as you start to understand marketing fundamentals, what marketing can achieve, and how it is implemented. The concepts are described briefly and concisely to enable you to cover a range of key material at first stage level. It does not attempt to be fully comprehensive, so to further develop your understanding of the concepts introduced here you should read widely from:

- The recommended course text (readings are specified for each of the Sessions in this book, and shown in Table 3 which follows).

- Other texts and workbooks listed in the syllabus reading list.

- The marketing press and national newspapers.

Other comprehensive marketing textbooks are detailed on the module reading list for the syllabus, and provide a wider context for the concepts explained in this Companion, and provide more Case Studies and examples to illustrate marketing in practice. The syllabus is available to registered students and members on the CIM Virtual Institute web site, www.cimvirtualinstitute.com.

The approach taken is a practical one of 'hands on'. The text explores what marketers in organisations do in a tactical role as assistants and junior practitioners. Each Session has a minimum of three activities with feedback given at the end of the Session, so readers can test their skills. Additional projects are suggested that involve some further research. No feedback is provided for these but the reader may wish to compare answers with other marketers studying at the same level.

Developing the skills to implement marketing activity

Equally important in the journey towards marketing excellence is the acquisition, development and refining of a range of skills that are required on a daily basis by marketers across all industries and sectors. These transferable skills hold the key to the effective implementation of the marketing techniques explored in this Companion. The focus of the practical activities contained in this book is on seven key business skills for marketers:

- Using ICT and the Internet.
- Using financial information and metrics.
- Presenting information.
- Working with others.
- Applying business law.
- Improving and developing own learning.
- Problem solving.

The first five of these key skills are linked to the activities shown in Table 1 which follows.

Improving and developing own learning is achieved by undertaking the projects that are at the end of each Session.

Problem solving is achieved through the Case Study and questions at the end of each Session.

Using the Companion

The syllabus for the module has been broken down into twelve Sessions, each of which is themed to help the student target different subjects from the syllabus. Marketing in Practice is generally studied last as it draws on the knowledge gained in other modules, so the student should refer back to other Companions at this level if he/she is unsure of underpinning theory at any stage. Every student brings with them to their studies different levels of experience, as a customer, from previous studies, and possibly from working in marketing or sales. As a student you should therefore be aware that, whilst you may need to spend considerable time on an unfamiliar area of the syllabus, you may make up this time when studying another area with which you are more familiar.

Each Session has a series of short Activities, which you should try to complete as you work your way through the text. These will help you to check your understanding of the material, and brief feedback is provided at the end of each Session, so that you can compare your answers.

At the end of each Session there is also a Case Study and a series of related questions. The Case Studies have been selected to illustrate marketing in practice so the questions help you to explore the issues raised. Try to complete these without reference to your notes, or the Session text, and then compare your answers with some key points that are given at the end of the Companion, in Appendix 1. The answers give limited feedback and should not be regarded as specimen answers for exam questions.

Finally, you will see that there is a specimen examination paper in Appendix 3. This can help you with your revision, examination technique, and preparation. Allow time nearer to your actual examination to complete the paper under examination conditions – that is, allow three hours of uninterrupted time, and complete the paper without reference to your notes or the study material. When you have completed the exercise, you can compare your answers to the notes in Appendix 4. If either your approach to the exercise, or the comparison of your answers highlight areas of particular weakness, you should refer back to the text and re-read the relevant Session, together with the chapters of the supporting textbook.

The practical nature of the syllabus for Marketing in Practice means that some learning outcomes are developed in more than one Session of the Companion.

The Companion starts by discussing how marketers develop effective relationships, internal and external to their organisation. In a marketing role you are involved in gathering information from many sources and presenting this verbally and in written format, so Sessions 3 and 4 discuss this section of the syllabus. Making use of this information to identify markets and promotional opportunities is covered in later Sessions.

The next two Sessions cover the organising of marketing events. Setting objectives and planning techniques are explored in Session 5, while Session 6 reviews the organising of different events such as exhibitions, conferences, meetings, seminars and press conferences. Session 7 discusses how to select and schedule media including the production of leaflets and brochures.

Sessions 8, 9 and 10 discuss co-ordinating the marketing mix while the final two Sessions lead the marketer through planning, preparing and presenting budgets.

Table 1 – Key skills

	Using ICT and Internet	Using financial information and metrics	Presenting information	Working with others	Applying business law	Improving and developing own learning	Problem solving
Session 1	1.4	1.3	1.2	1.1	1.5	Project activities	Case Study
Session 2	–	–	2.2, 2.3	2.1	2.4	Project activities	Case Study
Session 3	3.1	–	3.2, 3.5	3.4	3.3	Project activities	Case Study
Session 4	–	4.3	4.1	4.2	4.4	Project activities	Case Study
Session 5	5.2	5.4	5.3	5.1	–	Project activities	Case Study
Session 6	6.2	6.3	6.1	6.4	–	Project activities	Case Study
Session 7	7.2	7.3	7.1, 7.5	7.4	–	Project activities	Case Study
Session 8	–	8.1, 8.2	8.3	–	8.4	Project activities	Case Study
Session 9	9.2	–	9.1	9.4	9.3	Project activities	Case Study
Session 10	10.4	–	10.2	10.1	10.3	Project activities	Case Study
Session 11	11.5	11.2, 11.4	11.3	11.1	–	Project activities	Case Study
Session 12	–	12.2	12.1	–	–	Project activities	Case Study

Table 2 – Web sites

CIM	
www.cim.co.uk	The Chartered Institute of Marketing.
www.connectedinmarketing.com/cim/index.cfm	Everything you need to know about e-marketing.
www.cimvirtualinstitute.com	Key learning tool for CIM students.
General Marketing	
www.new-marketing.org	Research updates into new marketing issues, customer segmentation and repercussions for marketing practitioners.
www.wnim.com	What's new in marketing.
Advertising	
www.adslogans.co.uk	Online database of advertising slogans enabling marketers to check whether a slogan is already in use.
www.nielson-netratings.com	Details on current banner advertising.
www.ipa.co.uk	Institute of Practitioners in Advertising.
www.asa.org.uk	Advertising Standards Agency.
www.warc.com	Advertising and marketing related data, trends, etc.
Direct Marketing	
www.dma.org.uk	Direct Marketing Association.
www.theidm.co.uk	Institute of Direct Marketing.
E-marketing	
www.connectedinmarketing.com/ece/cfml/index.cfm	Everything you need to know about e-marketing.
www.shopping.yahoo.com	Browse retail sites.
www.ecommercetimes.com	Daily e-news.
www.amazon.com	Customer focused operation.
Events	
www.e-bulletin.com	Guide to exhibitions, events and resources.
www.venuefinder.com	International venue and event suppliers directory.
Sales Promotion	
www.isp.org.uk	Institute of Sales Promotion.

Public Relations	
www.prnewswire.co.uk	UK media monitoring service – reviews mentions in all media types (print, online publications and broadcast).
www.prsource.co.uk	PR and marketing information sources.
www.ipr.org.uk	Institute of Public Relations.
Personal Selling	
www.iops.co.uk	Institute of Professional Sales.
http://mkt.cba.cmich.edu/jpssm/	Journal of Personal Selling & Sales Management (American).
Marketing Research & Intelligence	
www.mrs.org.uk	The Market Research Society.
www.keynote.co.uk	Market research reports.
www.verdict.co.uk	Retail research reports.
www.datamonitor.com	Market analysis providing global data collection and in-depth analysis across any industry.
www.store.eiu.com	Economist Intelligence Unit providing country-specific global business analysis.
www.mintel.com	Consumer market research.
www.royalmail.co.uk	General marketing advice and information.
www.ft.com	Financial Times online newspaper and archives.
www.afxpress.com	Business news plus industry trends.
www.caci.co.uk	ACORN classification of residential neighbourhoods.
www.isi.gov.uk	Information society site with details of government projects, pending legislation etc.
www.worldmarketing.org	World Marketing Association.
www.statistics.gov.uk	Office for national statistics (UK).
www.homeoffice.gov.uk	Research development statistics.
www.business.com	Business search engine.
Legislation/Codes of Conduct	
www.wapforum.org	Industry association responsible for creating the standards for Wireless Application Protocol (WAP).

Table 3 – Background reading

The following references are suggested background readings for each Session. It is suggested that the student undertake this reading before studying the relevant Companion Session. Reading from additional texts is also required, particularly for the Sessions that have no specific reading from the core text. Please see relevant syllabus on CIM web site.

Session	Reading from Core Text : Dibb, Simkin, Pride & Ferrell: *Marketing concepts and strategies* (4th European Edition), Houghton Mifflin
Session 1	Chapter 1 – An Overview of the Marketing Concept. Chapter 23 – Organising Marketing Activities.
Session 2	Chapter 2 – The Marketing Environment from page 59. Chapter 5 – Organisational Markets and Business to Business Buying behaviour.
Session 3	Chapter 6 – Marketing Research and Information Systems.
Session 4	Chapter 7 – Segmenting Markets, Targeting and Positioning.
Session 5	No additional specific reading from core text.
Session 6	No additional specific reading from core text.
Session 7	Chapter 16 – Advertising, Public Relations and Sponsorship – from page 492.
Session 8	Chapter 8 – Product Decisions. Chapter 9 – Branding and Packaging. Chapter 10 – Developing and Managing products. Chapter 12 – Marketing Channels. Chapter 13 – Wholesalers, Distributors and Physical Distribution.
Session 9	Chapter 15 – Promotion: An Overview. Chapter 16 – Advertising, Public Relations and Sponsorship. Chapter 17 – Personal Selling, Sales Promotion, the Internet and Direct Marketing. Chapter 18 – Pricing Concepts. Chapter 19 – Setting Prices. Chapter 24 – Managing Ethics and Social Responsibility.
Session 10	Chapter 11 – The Marketing of Services.
Session 11	No additional specific reading from core text.
Session 12	No additional specific reading from core text.

Table 4 – Marketing models

The text in the Companion Sessions refers to a range of appropriate marketing models and examples of practical marketing, but does not reproduce these as they can be found in the core textbooks. The references for these are supplied in the following table. Models are used to simplify various complex situations or processes.

Session	Marketing Model	Reference: Dibb, Simkin, Pride & Ferrell: *Marketing concepts and strategies* (4th European Edition), Houghton Mifflin
Session 1	■ Marketing concept. ■ Advertising agency structure. ■ Structure of marketing function.	■ Page 9. ■ Page 505. ■ Page 721/722.
Session 2	■ Macro/micro environment. ■ b2b buying/relationships.	■ Page 60. ■ Page 153/154.
Session 3	■ Sources of secondary information. ■ Managing information. ■ Data collection (secondary). ■ Example of secondary information. ■ Graphical presentation of information.	■ Page 78. ■ Page 170/171. ■ Page 178. ■ Page 539/546/550. ■ Page 706.
Session 4	■ Socio-economic classification. ■ Market segmentation approach. ■ Basic elements of segmentation. ■ Segmenting consumer markets. ■ Example of life cycle stages. ■ ACORN. ■ Segmenting b2b markets. ■ Target market strategy.	■ Page 130/131. ■ Page 206. ■ Page 209. ■ Page 211. ■ Page 215. ■ Page 217. ■ Page 224. ■ Page 231.

Session	Marketing Model	Reference: Dibb, Simkin, Pride & Ferrell: *Marketing concepts and strategies* (4th European Edition), Houghton Mifflin
Session 5	■ Advertising media. ■ Elements of artwork. ■ Advertisement techniques.	■ Page 496-498. ■ Page 500. ■ Page 502.
Session 6	■ Example of plan. ■ Venue comparisons.	■ Page 694. ■ Page 719.
Session 7	■ Analysis of activities.	■ Page 514.
Session 8	■ Levels of product. ■ Product mix and depth. ■ PLC. ■ Brand equity. ■ NPD. ■ Product deletion. ■ Product adoption. ■ Channel intermediaries. ■ Types of channel. ■ Push/Pull strategies. ■ Channel sales promotion.	■ Page 254. ■ Page 256. ■ Page 258. ■ Page 273. ■ Page 299. ■ Page 312. ■ Page 462. ■ Page 353/354. ■ Page 357/359/622. ■ Page 472. ■ Page 538.
Session 9	■ Uses of advertising. ■ Criteria for advertising. ■ AIDA. ■ Topics for press releases. ■ Pricing decisions. ■ Establishing prices. ■ Promotional pricing. ■ Example of Code of Ethics. ■ Model of social corporate responsibility. ■ Social responsibility issues.	■ Page 483. ■ Page 488. ■ Page 499. ■ Page 509. ■ Page 573/575. ■ Page 589. ■ Page 603. ■ Page 767. ■ Page 769. ■ Page 770.

Session	Marketing Model	Reference: Dibb, Simkin, Pride & Ferrell: *Marketing concepts and strategies* (4th European Edition), Houghton Mifflin
Session 10	■ Classification of services. ■ Dimensions of service quality. ■ Elements of personal selling.	■ Page 326. ■ Page 331/332. ■ Page 524.
Session 11	■ Example of expenditure. ■ Costs and their relationships. ■ Break-even. ■ P & L statement.	■ Page 514. ■ Page 595/597. ■ Page 598. ■ Page 745.
Session 12	■ Example of expenditure and results.	■ Page 555.

Session 1

The marketing function

Introduction

This Session explores the 'who's who' in marketing and how the marketing function interacts with other organisational functions. The marketing plan is derived from the overall business objectives so marketing personnel need to communicate, and share information with, other people and departments.

Developing productive working relationships within the marketing function, across the organisation and externally, demands good interpersonal skills and the ability to communicate effectively. This is explored in this first Session and continued in the next, which reviews the front-line role and the development of relevant networks of contacts.

LEARNING OUTCOMES

At the end of this Session you will be able to:

- Describe the structure and roles of the marketing function in both small and large organisations.

- Understand how to build and develop relationships within the marketing department.

- Appreciate how to work effectively with others, including your manager.

- Explain the concept of e-relationships.

Marketing oriented companies

In a marketing oriented company, regardless of size, satisfying the customer is regarded as the route to success and profitability. Resources are allocated to activities designed to find out what the customer needs so that products and services can be provided to meet those requirements. The prevailing culture enhances effective customer-supplier relationships so internal and external customer needs are met. Marketers must establish good working relationships with colleagues in other organisational functions to promote the sharing of information and ideas. This ensures that cross-functional problems are identified and solved as quickly as possible.

Marketers are often the 'voice' of the organisation to the media so they need to develop an internal network of contacts to ensure they are fully informed and up-to-date with all organisational activities and policies. Alternatively, marketers working in PR may be required to brief other functional managers preparing for a press or broadcast interview to ensure that what they say 'fits' with other corporate communications.

Similar to the other functions of the organisation, the overall marketing objectives are derived from the business objectives. However, each function will have a different viewpoint and there is potential for conflict. For example, in a manufacturing company, Purchasing and Finance will want to simplify administration and minimise costs, so will prefer to buy large quantities of raw materials from a limited range of suppliers. This means that they will be in a powerful position to negotiate discounts for large orders and other benefits like 'just in time' delivery. Marketing may want to be more flexible in order to meet individual customers' specific needs, so prefer to buy from a larger range of suppliers.

Activity 1.1: Function v function?

In a manufacturing company what potential conflicts might exist between:

i)   Marketing and Production?

ii)   Marketing and Accounts?

Structure of the marketing function

In large organisations, marketing is represented at board level by the Marketing Director, who is responsible for developing marketing objectives and strategy. This role is often supported by a PA and Marketing Manager who co-ordinates and controls operations. Both the Marketing Manager and Director may be generalists, whereas other roles will probably be taken by specialists, such as the PR or Communications Manager and Brand Manager.

Managers usually lead a team of marketing executives and assistants who carry out operational and tactical activities.

Typical specialist roles and main responsibilities are outlined below.

Marketing research manager:
- Gathers, collates and disseminates information for marketing decisions.
- Works with external agencies to design marketing research.

PR or communications manager:
- Advises senior management on PR opportunities.
- Reports on PR activities and maintains a library of press cuttings and photographs.
- Represents the company when a spokesperson is required.
- Co-ordinates corporate public affairs.
- Co-ordinates the production of all internal and external corporate communications.
- Advises on media selection – including assessing the benefits of new technologies.

Advertising manager:
- Plans and co-ordinates advertising campaigns.
- Works with external advertising and media specialists.
- Evaluates and advises on new media opportunities such as Internet.

Direct marketing manager:
- Generates direct mailings and marketing activities.
- Maintains customer databases.
- Advises on customer loyalty programmes.

Events manager:
- Plans and co-ordinates marketing events such as exhibitions, product launches and meetings.
- Organises corporate hospitality.
- Recruits and trains staff required to work at special events.

Product manager:

- Controls all activities, such as sales promotions, relating to a specific product range to maximise sales.

- Monitors product trends.

- May report to the Product Director if the company structure is organised around Product Divisions.

Research and development manager (product development manager):

- Heads up R&D team.

- Responsible for new product development.

Brand manager:

- Controls and protects brand image.

- Advises on branding activities.

- Assesses impact of rival brands.

It can be seen from the above that many activities are interrelated; for example, advertising, branding and activities relating to promotion of products. Thus the number of specialists in smaller organisations will be considerably less. The marketing function may consist of several managers who cover all activities. One or all may report to the company board and Marketing Director. In some small organisations roles will be shared so that one individual is responsible for marketing and sales, for example.

Activity 1.2: Who's who?

Draw a typical structure for the marketing department of a small- to medium-sized IT software company.

The activities carried out by the marketing function include product promotion, market research, development of new products, company image and branding.

Giving internal briefings

Briefings are different to meetings. Briefings are used to pass on information so there is little or no debate and discussion. Usually, questions are taken at the end by the person giving the briefing, and limited to the topic of the briefing – to ensure all have understood.

There are many occasions on which you might attend a briefing or give one yourself. These might be:

- Final product launch briefing – everyone involved is brought together before the event to be given information about the programme, individual roles and responsibilities, number and characteristics of visitors, arrangements for media and other essential details so they know what is to happen.

- Exhibition briefing – at the start of each day of the event, staff on the stand come together to be told the programme for the day and when refreshment breaks are, how to deal with visitors, details about any special activities or visitors to the event that have been arranged by the exhibition organisers and other details that ensure that they make the best of the opportunities to develop sales leads or make sales.

Briefings should be as short as possible but the information must be presented in a clear way. Written instructions must be provided so attendees have future reference material if they need to check any details. There is no set pattern but the following checklist is helpful when briefing staff before an event:

- Event objectives – reminders of what the organisation needs to achieve and how this will be measured.

- Progress to date – brief summary.

- Programme – details of scheduled activities and timings.

- Venue and facilities – relevant details such as venue plan.

- Equipment to be used – audio visual arrangements for speeches etc.

- Roles and responsibilities – people need to know what they are doing as individuals and how that fits with the tasks that others are carrying out.

- Potential problems – what might go wrong and how this can be avoided.

- Visitor characteristics – numbers, status (celebrity, royalty etc.), nationality and other relevant facts.

- Hosting arrangements – greeting and directing attendees, catering, recording details of visitors.

- Event materials – what written information will be supplied.

- Publicity – how this will be handled.

- Rehearsal – is a 'dress rehearsal' required for presentations or other activities?

- What to do at the close and immediately following the event.

There will also be special arrangements that are specific to that event so it is important that a project plan is developed at the earliest stage. This is discussed in Sessions 5 and 6 on planning and organising marketing events.

Activity 1.3: How well did it really go?

Evaluating the success of marketing activities is important because it helps identify whether money has been invested wisely, and provides information for future planning.

Why do you think it is more effective to measure achievement over a period of time following an event, rather than only immediately after the event?

Working with external agencies

Marketers need to understand company business objectives, values and policies in order to interact with other functions and communicate effectively, internally and externally. Marketing supports other functions and is supported by them but, as has already been mentioned, potential for conflict exists. All functions must share ideas and information if they are to co-operate and 'pull in the same direction'. Each must understand the other's viewpoint and what the company needs to do to achieve the overall business objectives if functional objectives, operations and tactics are consistent.

This knowledge is also important when dealing with external agencies. Organisations tend to deal with many external agencies including suppliers, intermediaries and media, local community and government officials and consumer groups. At all meetings, negotiations and when in communication with people outside the organisation, marketers are acting as a representative for that company. Therefore, they must be aware of the approach they must take and what is important to the organisation.

Media briefings are explored in Session 7 on working with the media.

Negotiating with suppliers and intermediaries is discussed in Session 2.

Working with external agencies

Taking time at the start to select the right agency to work with is time well spent. The agency must be capable of interpreting briefs correctly and producing work that fits the image the organisation wishes to communicate. This means developing a long-term relationship so both parties get to know each other well and learn how to work together efficiently and effectively.

Working with an agency is a process that includes:

- Research – interview a number of agencies and ask each to make a presentation about 'what they can do for you'.

- Shortlisting – prepare a list of those agencies you feel you will be able to work with and invite them to complete a small project to demonstrate quality of work.

- Decision – the right people (including those who will be working with the agency) need to be involved in making the final choice.

- Appointment – agree terms and conditions so each party knows what is expected and required of them.

- Monitoring and review – monitor the performance of the agency and review the cost-effectiveness with them periodically.

When starting the process it is useful to ask for references so you can talk to organisations that have used the agency.

Activity 1.4: Hide and seek?

When selecting external agencies it is a good idea to look at their web site to see how user friendly it is. Look at the following web sites and note how easy it is to find what you are looking for.

- Exhibition Bulletin   www.e-bulletin.com

- Direct Marketing Association   www.dma.org.uk

- Marketing Week Magazine   www.mad.co.uk

Working with others

From the above it can be appreciated that marketers deal extensively with agencies outside the organisation. Sometimes this is to pass on information, but it may be to negotiate with suppliers or to brief advertising agencies. In all such work it is important that the marketer is able to work effectively with other people. The main skills required to develop good working relationships are outlined below.

Skill	Application
Communication.	Questioning and listening skills to gather information, good command of language to articulate argument and take part in discussion, openness and integrity.
Presentation.	Presenting a business case clearly and concisely.
Teamworking.	Supporting others and developing their ideas, taking the lead when required, being aware of others' problems and helping to solve these appropriately, supporting decisions made by the group.
Observation.	Taking care to find out how others feel and watching impact of own behaviour on others.
Problem solving and decision making.	Contributing effectively to the process, sharing relevant information and being able to evaluate options before making a final decision.
Negotiation.	Willingness to look for a win-win situation while understanding what own side needs to achieve.
Assertiveness.	Being clear about what you want while respecting the rights of others.
Ethical behaviour.	Understanding each party's set of values and ensuring that personal actions do not compromise these.
Managing self.	Organising workload to meet deadlines, being punctual for appointments and being reliable.

Figure 1.1: Key skills for effective working relationships

Working with your own manager

This is a two-way relationship that should be built on trust, respect, openness and honesty. The marketer relies on the manager for guidance, support and direction while the manager needs the marketer to complete work accurately, on time and to make suggestions for improvements to the way of working.

Reporting progress and achievements to your line manager is an important part of the relationship. Good practice covers:

- Accuracy – check facts and figures are correct and up to date.
- Proactivity – identify barriers to achievement and present solutions.
- Consultation – ask for advice or additional support as soon as it is required.
- Continuous improvement – make suggestions for better ways of working.
- Response – seek feedback and act upon it.
- Understanding – ask questions and listen to ensure you know what is required.
- Empathy – try to put yourself in your line manager's shoes, especially when he/she says no to a request.

If there is disagreement, then it is the responsibility of both parties to look for a constructive solution so the relationship is enhanced not destroyed. Furthermore, the marketer should also seek opportunities to learn new skills and practise newly acquired abilities. Being willing to take on extra responsibilities enables you to develop within your current role and makes you more employable within the organisation.

E-relationships

The digital revolution has created opportunities for people to communicate and develop remote relationships. Email is a regular means of sharing information and ideas for many customers and suppliers, marketing team members and other organisational functions due to the speed at which information is transmitted and received and the convenience factor. The main limitations are that the communication is open to misinterpretation because valuable clues to meaning, such as tone of voice and body language, are absent.

E-relationships are convenient because time, distance and organisation are no barrier to communication. However, simply sending an email or reply does not absolve the sender from responsibility. You do not know if the message has been received and understood until the required action or response is elicited. Therefore, if it is an important communication you might need to telephone to check if it has been received and understood. Requesting an automatic response only guarantees it has been received.

Examples of the use of electronic communication to develop relationships in marketing include:

- Extranets – for example, letting the supplier have access to part of the company Intranet to check when raw materials are running low so more supplies can be sent. In this case it is usual for both parties to have agreed the level to which materials are to be maintained by the supplier.

- E-commerce – the customer can purchase online 24/7. However, the customer has to be in to receive delivery and is usually required to pick up the phone if something goes wrong.

Activity 1.5: What is the law?

How much do you know about Internet advertising and the law, in particular data protection legislation covering the storage and use of personal information?

Where, on the Internet, do you think you could find some information to provide guidance for e-tailers (organisations offering goods for sale on the Internet)?

Case Study – The weakest link?

There's so much talk about the importance of service and customer empowerment, that it would be easy to assume that brand owners are bending over backwards to please their customers. However, marketers are often guilty of causing more confusion than delight!

Confusion marketing is a problem common in the early stages of a brand's life – in the way it is positioned and sold to the consumer. Pricing, design and advertising are all areas where marketers can be guilty of much skullduggery and deception. But what about after the sale is made, when the customer gets the product home? Now that the complicated buying process is over, the customer can get down to the simple pleasure of enjoying the product. Or perhaps not.

Unfortunately this is when maximum confusion can arise and, to make matters worse, it is also when the company, having tried so hard to get its product into the customer's hands, makes a run for it. For all the rhetoric about customer relationship management and lifetime customer value, the fact is that many companies are still more focused on pushing products into consumers' hands than they are in turning sales into relationships. Whether it is something as simple as providing clear instructions about how a product works, making it easy for customers to get answers to problems or explaining changes to the product or company, marketers often lose interest in the post-sale 'afterlife'.

There are many examples. Internet service providers promise a certain level of service, fail to deliver and then make it extremely difficult for customers to get information that will help them. Helplines charged at premium rates and customers promised unlimited surf time only to be expelled from the service because they are using it too much have been common in the past. Post-sale confusion in financial services has led the Financial Services Authority (FSA) to begin compiling a report called 'Treating customers fairly after the point of sale' in which it extends its previous remit of looking at sales tactics to focus on how customers are treated after they have bought a product. Poor standards of ongoing communication and explanation to customers about their options, prompted the FSA to investigate post-sale confusion in more detail.

The FSA says examples of the activities it wants to stamp out include banks and lenders who do not keep long-term customers informed of improved products and deals which might benefit them. It has been reported that banks and mortgage companies sometimes withhold new savings rates or repayment plans from long-standing customers, preferring to hold back the best deals for new prospects.

Mick McTeer, senior policy adviser with the Consumers Association, is not surprised at this activity. He says, "Financial services brands have no incentive to tell existing customers about new deals. It's not in their interests to do so, as it only draws attention to how poor their product was in the first place. Instead, they make the product as complex as possible and hope the customer decides it's too difficult to switch."

However, efforts are being made to inject simplicity into financial services and make ongoing communication with customers an opportunity instead of a threat. Virgin Direct was one of the first to go down this route and, in its bid to demystify money, it saw post-sale communication as a key area to tackle. Communications Manager, Andrew Stronach, explains; "We saw that the industry put a lot of effort into getting the customer through the door, but after that, there was little contact.

An annual statement on your pension or mortgage was the best you could hope for. Also, the role of brokers confuses customers even more, making them unsure about who to go to if they have a problem. The result is that a lot of companies are expert at dealing with brokers but useless at communicating with customers."

Virgin's answer was to make itself available as a single point of contact at all times of day and via whatever channel of communication – be it the phone or the web –that the customer preferred to use. So, even though you might find a better pension or mortgage than by going to Virgin, the brand attracts business by being open and honest.

Source: *Marketing Business*, April 2001.

Questions

1. What are the implications of confusion marketing for organisations that are marketing oriented?

2. How can organisations assess if they are treating their customers 'fairly' at the point of sale?

3. What else could companies like Virgin, who offer financial services, do to avoid confusion marketing?

SUMMARY OF KEY POINTS

- In effective organisations the marketing function communicates with other functions to ensure consistent and coherent implementation of business objectives and company policies and procedures.

- The structure of the marketing function varies according to the size of the organisation. In small organisations individuals will be responsible for a number of roles whereas large organisations will have people in role-specific jobs.

- Marketers interact with a large number of people, internal and external to their organisation, so need to develop skills that will help them build effective working relationships.

- When selecting external agencies, determine selection criteria that include screening, shortlisting and sampling to make the right decision.

- The use of email and other electronic forms of communication have increased the speed and availability of information and contact but reduced personal contact, which may have a negative impact on the development of close working relationships.

Improving and developing own learning

The following projects are designed to help you to develop your knowledge and skills further by carrying out some research yourself. Feedback is not provided for this type of learning because there are no 'answers' to be found, but you may wish to discuss your findings with colleagues and fellow students.

Project A

For your own organisation, or one you know well, investigate the structure of the marketing department and draw a chart to show the different roles and how they interact. This may not be as straightforward as Activity 1.2 if it is a large organisation and people work in several different teams, some of which may be cross functional (composed of people from different functions).

For the same organisation, note the main external agencies they deal with. Why are these agencies used?

Project B

Review the list of skills in the section on 'Working with others' and carry out a personal audit of abilities.

What areas do you feel strong in and where do you think there is room for improvement?

What opportunities can you identify to help you develop the additional skills you need to work more effectively with others?

How effectively do you work with your manager?

Do you think that the relationship can be improved?

How might this be achieved?

Project C

Look at the following supermarket web sites that offer consumers the opportunity to shop online.

www.tesco.com
www.sainsburys.co.uk
www.asda.co.uk

How do you feel as a customer not having personal contact with the organisation or being able to touch the goods prior to delivery?

Feedback on activities

Activity 1.1: Function v function?

i) Marketing and production

In order to meet a customer's exact requirements Marketing might need short production runs which are inefficient and uneconomic for production.

ii) Marketing and accounts

Similar to other administration activities, Accounts will prefer standard transactions to minimise time spent on individual accounts. However, Marketing again might want to be more flexible and give different discounts and terms to different customers. They may wish to reward loyal customers to encourage further loyalty or give an incentive discount to a new customer.

Activity 1.2: Who's who?

In a small or medium sized company, marketing and sales might be located in the same department as there needs to be significant interaction between the two functions. In larger organisations they are more likely to be separated. The assumption for this activity is that the organisation is of sufficient size to require a number of specialists. However, in Small to Medium size Enterprises (SMEs) there would be few or no specialists; simply marketing generalists who cover the full range of activities required.

Typical structure might look like this:

Activity 1.3: How well did it really go?

Measuring immediately following the event will give a good idea of success but may not be valid in the future. For example, counting the number of sales leads from an exhibition will provide a number but some of those may not be converted. The quality of the leads will only be revealed if measured at a later date. Real sales leads will have turned into sales, so a more reliable measurement of success is made. If none are converted then it may be that it was not the right place to promote the product.

Activity 1.4: Hide and seek?

Good web site design ensures that the customer is able to find what he/she is looking for quickly and easily. This means that the home page must be clearly constructed to show what the supplier does and how to find out about it. An effective site map is of greater benefit to the customer than impressive graphics that take a long time to download. Other useful features include good links to help navigation, a search facility, contact details, clear and concise catalogue, company history and frequently asked questions.

Activity 1.5: What is the law?

Check out the Advertising Standards Agency (ASA) www.asa.org.uk for details on self-regulation. Go the section on 'Codes' and click on legislation to view the legal framework that advertiser should refer to when designing advertisements.

The Internet is not a broadcast medium and is difficult to regulate but it is advisable for advertisers to be aware of the codes of conduct set by the self-regulatory body, the ASA. As a global medium it is particularly difficult to regulate because it is not clear under which country's laws an offender should be prosecuted.

The law is changing constantly so it is advisable always to seek legal advice from an expert when publishing material in any medium.

Session 2

Effective working relationships

Introduction

People in front-line roles are company representatives whenever they interact with customers or external agencies. They are part of the way the organisation communicates externally. The skills required are similar to those discussed previously but this Session also considers the importance of non-verbal communication and the cultural considerations of dealing with international visitors.

Dealing with suppliers on behalf of the organisation also requires specific knowledge and skills such as relationship building, awareness of contract law and negotiation. Finally, networking and the skills needed to network effectively in the marketing and business worlds are examined.

The marketer in a front-line role must be a skilled communicator, have good interpersonal skills and enjoy meeting new people.

LEARNING OUTCOMES

At the end of this Session you will be able to:

- Represent the organisation using practical public relations skills.

- Understand the practical aspects of working in a front-line role, particularly receiving and assisting visitors.

- Understand how to deal efficiently with internal and external enquiries.

- Identify relevant cultural considerations when receiving and assisting international visitors and agencies.

- Explain how the organisation fits into a supply chain and works with distribution channels.

- Explain the supplier interface: negotiating, collaborating, operational and contractual aspects.

- Use networking skills in the business world.

Representing the company

The previous Session discussed why it is essential that marketers understand the business of the organisation and company policies. When representing the organisation it is important that the message communicated by people at the front-line is consistent with company image and values.

For example, if the organisation has a reputation for exceptionally high standards of service for individuals, then customers need to experience that at every point of contact from the ordering of a product to delivery and after-sales service. That level of service may be a key factor in customer retention. If loyal customers visiting an exhibition are dealt with in an offhand manner by staff on the stand, then all previous good work may be wasted. Research shows that poor service is a major reason why organisations lose customers.

There are many situations where marketers will find themselves representing their organisation. These include press conferences, product launches, corporate hospitality events, exhibitions, hosting visits to the organisation and dealing with customers, suppliers and other external agencies.

In addition to the skills described in the section on 'Working with others' in Session 1, when working face to face marketers need to consider:

- **Appearance**

  First impressions are what people will use to judge you and your organisation. Therefore, you need to wear appropriate dress at all time. This might be professional, business attire or so-called 'smart casual'. If in doubt, check with a senior colleague. Many organisations supply uniforms or have a strict dress code to ensure that first impressions are favourable and in-line with company image.

  Of course, it is essential that front-line staff are clean and tidy at all times – don't forget shoes. If worn, accessories such as jewellery should be discreet.

- **Body language**

  When meeting or greeting a visitor or customer, that person will form an impression of you before you speak. There's an old saying that you don't get a second chance to make a first impression. The non-verbal clues that communicate messages include the gestures you make with your hands, the way you stand or sit and how you hold your head.

You may appear:

Overbearing or aggressive if you –
Bang the table, stare, look over your spectacles, raise your eyebrows in disbelief, point your finger, smile knowingly ("heard it all before") or stand over the person and look down on him/her.

Disinterested or bored if you –
Do not make eye contact but look around the room, shuffle paper or play with a pen on the desk in front of you, fidget and sigh.

Uncomfortable, perhaps defensive if you –
Continually rub your eyes, nose or ears, keep looking away, fold your arms, clench your fists, sit back in your chair and cross your legs.

Over-anxious if you –
Keep chewing your finger or licking your lips, continually clear your throat, blink excessively, pull on your ear lobe and shuffle around a lot in your chair.

Whereas, you should appear:

Ready to help and alert if you –
Smile in a friendly manner, look directly at the person and make good eye contact, smile pleasantly, demonstrate that you are listening by nodding as they speak, appear interested by leaning towards them slightly and adopt an open posture when standing or sitting.

Thoughtful and interested if you –
Rest your chin on your hand or pinch the bridge of your nose, tilt your head to one side and lean towards the person when speaking but lean back to listen.

Confident if you –
Maintain good eye contact, blink naturally, smile pleasantly and nod when listening.

You should also be aware of the non-verbal clues that the other person is communicating. However, body language, like other messages, is open to interpretation, so when communicating face to face do not judge a person on a single gesture or action. Look for clusters of behaviour that are consistent and so suggest that the person may be interested and alert, or perhaps bored or defensive, and respond accordingly.

Ensure that your own body language supports your verbal communication because the non-verbal clues you give have a higher weighting than the content of the message when speaking face to face. The receiver of your message will use the words you say, the tone of voice and body language in a ratio of around 10%, 35% and 55% respectively to 'decode' the communication.

■ **Etiquette**

This refers to the conventions of social behaviour and is particularly important when meeting and greeting people. Always check that names are correctly pronounced, people introduced in the correct order and the right form of address is used (Your Royal Highness etc.) This will also be discussed later in the section on 'Hosting visitors from overseas'.

■ **Speech**

All verbal communication must be spoken clearly so everyone can hear. If people have a disability then make sure you understand their special needs so you can communicate as effectively with them as others. Use appropriate language and tone of voice. Make sure you are interested in the other person. If you feel that you don't care, that feeling will be reflected in your voice and manner.

If you are unsure of your abilities in a given situation use positive inner dialogue to give yourself more confidence. In other words talk to yourself in a positive manner about what you are going to do and how you are going to do it. Do not convince yourself that you will not be able to cope – otherwise it will come true!

■ **Attitude**

Attitude cannot be seen but the effects can be observed in behaviour. For example, if a salesperson feels that you are not really interested in the product he/she is selling then this will be evident in the presentation. The salesperson will not put much effort into finding out about what the customer wants and trying to ensure that those needs will be met by the product.

You cannot help your inner thoughts or attitude but you can control your actions. Even if you feel de-motivated, you must be a professional in the front-line role and show a positive, friendly and helpful attitude towards customers and visitors at all times.

Activity 2.1: Showing that you care

You are preparing a customer care training session for front-line staff.

Think about the types of behaviour that staff need to employ when dealing with the customer.

Write a checklist that they can use for self-assessment.

Dealing with enquiries

A significant part of a marketer's time will be spent on dealing with enquiries from both internal and external customers and agencies. If the enquiry cannot be answered then it must be passed to the right person immediately so it is dealt with as soon as possible. In this case, explain to the enquirer who that will be and when that individual will respond.

If it is a telephone enquiry then try to connect the enquirer with the member of staff who can help straightaway. Take details of the problem and give these to the organisational contact before passing the enquirer on so they do not have to repeat what they have already said. If you have to ring back with the information, prepare what you are going to say in case you have to leave a message.

When talking to people by telephone it is impossible to observe their body language. Therefore the receiver uses content and tone of voice to interpret the message.

Activity 2.2: Ring, ring!

For the same training course as in Activity 2.1, write two sets of guidelines for staff dealing with people on the telephone. Present the information as bulleted lists:

- Good practice when talking on the telephone.

- How to avoid problems when dealing with telephone callers.

Assertive behaviour

Assertive people are more effective, vital and valued in today's changing and demanding environment. In a front-line role it is important to listen to others but also to stand up for what is right. That is being assertive so long as other people's rights are also respected. Aggressive people are intolerant of what others want and often do not care so long as they 'get their own way'.

When dealing with visitors, they may make difficult demands. For example, if hosting a corporate visit someone might request a tour round a restricted area. Instead of saying 'No, that is not allowed', which might be interpreted as aggressive, it is better to say, 'I understand why you would find it interesting to see that department. Unfortunately, it not possible to organise that but I can arrange for the manager in charge to come and talk to you about the work that goes on there'.

When being assertive:

1. Acknowledge the other person's point of view and demonstrate understanding.

2. Say what you feel.

3. State what you think should happen.

Applying these three simple rules enables you to show that the other person's point of view is important to you before saying what you want. Through listening to each other it is much more likely that the right course of action is agreed on rather than the stronger individual dominating the weaker.

Passive behaviour is as ineffective as aggressiveness. Individuals adopting this style of behaviour allow others to say what should happen and go along with the decision, even if it is not 'right' for them. They appear indecisive and lacking in confidence.

The following table identifies the three different types of behaviour so it is easy to see the benefits of assertiveness.

People behaving…

Assertively…	Aggressively…	Passively…
Protect their own rights and respect the rights of others.	Violate rights and take advantage of others.	Have their rights violated, so are taken advantage of.
Achieve goals without hurting others.	Probably achieve goals at the expense of others.	Do not achieve goals.
Feel good about themselves and are confident about abilities.	Are defensive, belligerent and humiliate others.	Feel frustrated, unhappy, anxious and are often hurt.
Are socially and emotionally expressive.	Can be explosive, unpredictable, hostile and angry.	Tend to be inhibited and withdrawn.
Make choices for themselves.	Intrude on other's choices.	Allow others to choose for them.

Figure 2.1: Effects of assertive, aggressive and passive behaviour

Hosting marketing events

This is also covered in Session 6 which explores some of the different types of activities that marketers organise and host.

When hosting a function or receiving visitors to an event, the following arrangements need to be made:

- Advance information must be sent to those attending giving details of the nature of the event, the programme of activities and contact numbers for enquiries.

- Venue and facilities booked.

- Refreshments confirmed and ordered.

- Event staff need to be selected and briefed – there may also be training requirements. (Staff include hospitality, catering, security and company representatives).
- Special arrangements need to be made for VIPs.
- Event programme must be checked and double checked with planners to make sure there are no last minute changes – perhaps due to a change of speaker.
- Event evaluation should be planned.

Hosting visitors from overseas

Different countries have different cultures, values and beliefs. This means that when hosting multi-cultural events a number of additional factors need to be considered:

- Language – printed materials may need to be produced in more than one language and interpreters may be required.
- Catering – some cultures do not permit the eating of certain foods or drink.
- Time zone differences – allow additional time for registration as delegates will be arriving over a longer period of time, and arrange start and finish times to fit in with rail and air timetables.
- Travel arrangements – make sure overseas visitors know how to reach the venue from train stations and airports, providing transport if appropriate.
- Provide cultural awareness training for front-line conference staff to include social structures of different countries, forms of greeting and different customs and practices.
- Organising the event may take longer due to delays communicating across borders – use Internet and email to speed this up.

Negotiating with suppliers and other external agencies

Marketers may have to deal with internal suppliers to the marketing department and external suppliers. When involved in negotiation, the marketer needs to gather information to help him/her prepare. This includes knowledge of any common ground. The same principles apply when dealing with internal and external suppliers, although dealings with internal suppliers may be less formal.

Within negotiations there are a number of recognisable stages. Once the openings have taken place and each party has agreed to observe certain rules of behaviour, negotiations begin:

- **Exploration**

  This first stage could also be termed the research phase. Each party states their position, priorities and identifies constraints. Initial impressions are important – negotiators need to listen to the other side and observe non-verbal clues carefully. Good eye contact is essential – a steady gaze suggests integrity whereas fidgeting and looking away might indicate to the other side that there is something to hide! Successful negotiators use assertive behaviour and appear confident in themselves and their ability to reach a win-win solution.

  Having determined each other's position both parties should then put forward a range of options for consideration. The benefits for each side need to be clear so the real 'value' of what is offered is evident. For example, the supplier may agree to a short lead time if the customer agrees a regular order size.

- **Framing or outlining the deal**

  Both parties need to make the other side understand what they must have – what is essential or preferred. Clarity of communication is important so verbal and non-verbal messages need to be aligned.

- **Bidding and counter bidding**

  A critical stage. If discussing price then start at the top (high but realistic) because the only way is down! Confident behaviour is recommended! The other side will respond with a low offer so the range for negotiation is set. This is the start of a game of 'give and take'. As options are put forward then other incentives might be introduced. For example, if the customer agrees to place a minimum size of order each time then the supplier might agree a larger discount.

- **Bargaining**

  The chief negotiator must understand his/her level of authority to agree to or offer different concessions. Uncertainty will not reassure the other side who may take advantage of any hesitancy to secure additional benefits for themselves.

If this stage is conducted in an open and friendly manner, then it augurs well for the development of a longer-term relationship. Using the same suppliers and external agencies produces many mutual benefits as both sides gain knowledge about each other's business requirements and can make recommendations for solving problems.

- **Closing**

  Summarise the negotiations and test understanding to make sure all involved are clear about what has been agreed. This ensures that when written confirmation is sent there are no surprises for either party.

  During negotiations it is important to display positive body language to show that there is nothing to hide. A quiet environment with no interruptions is required so people can listen carefully and calmly. Emotion introduces 'noise' so the receiver does not decode the original message accurately. Effective negotiators avoid aggressive or dismissive behaviour that may anger the other side.

The supply chain

Organisations deal with numerous suppliers, some directly and some through intermediaries as shown in the example below of a car manufacturer.

In this simple example, the gear boxes are manufactured by a supplier for the car manufacturer. Therefore, a chain exists and a problem with raw materials at the start of the chain will impact on the end of the chain. In addition, if the car manufacturer is looking for ways to cut costs and negotiates a lower price with the gear box supplier then that company relies on negotiating a lower price for raw materials or loses margin.

Activity 2.3: Communicating with suppliers

As marketing manager for The Shopper's Catalogue you and your team sell space to companies who wish to advertise their products in your catalogue. Following a telephone conversation with a valued customer you agreed to provide confirmation of the price offered.

Compose a suitable letter.

Entering into a contract

A contract, however carefully negotiated, should not be entered into lightly because it is legally binding, so neither party can be released from agreed commitments without the consent of the other. In addition, liabilities resulting from a breach of contract may exceed the original price of the goods or services being procured.

The contract does not have to be a written document – it can be a verbal agreement with the exception of contracts of guarantee, hire purchase and insurance. However, if the terms are not written down, then it is difficult to prove, at a later date, what the agreement was. Verbal arrangements can also appear casual and unprofessional – it is not simply a matter of the two parties not trusting one another.

In order for a contract to exist the following must be adhered to:

- Each party must intend to and communicate an intention to enter into a contract under the law.

- Following the offer made by one party the other must make an unqualified acceptance.

- Both parties must have the capacity to enter into the contract.

- Consent must be legally obtained – there must be no duress, misrepresentation, deceit or fraud, even if it is unintentional.

- The contract must not be for an immoral or illegal purpose.

- Both parties must be able to fulfil the obligations placed on them by the contract.

- There must be consideration – there must be payment for the goods or services.

A contract does not always have to be written, so you have to be careful not to enter into an implied or unwritten contract. If entering into a written contract with a supplier, read the terms and conditions very carefully and seek advice on any statements that appear unclear or are open to interpretation. Ignorance is no protection should anything go wrong in the future.

Frustration of contract

A contract is absolute, once both parties have accepted contractual obligations, which means that it cannot be argued at a later date by one party that later circumstances made it impossible for them to fulfil their obligations. However, frustration of contract may occur if subsequent events mean that the contractual obligations are radically different from when the contract was agreed. For example, if you hired a venue and it was destroyed by fire before your event, then the contract may be held to be frustrated.

In the event of possible frustration of contract seek legal advice immediately to test this out and make arrangements for any expenses paid or costs incurred to be recovered.

Activity 2.4: Frustration

Judge whether the following situations might lead to the frustration of the original contract:

i)   Booking a celebrity to appear at a corporate event who falls ill and is unable to attend due to that illness.

ii)   Hiring a marquee to host a hospitality event at an outdoor show that is cancelled by the organisers at short notice.

Networking

Networking in the business world means extending your relevant contacts so you know and are known by individuals and groups within your working environment who could help you in your work. Marketers working in PR will develop contacts within the media such as editors and journalists, so they are asked for quotes and know how to produce newsworthy communications that will achieve widespread coverage.

You already know a large number of people so are part of several networks. Consider your business network and review the different areas of your work where you have developed contacts. There are several ways that you will have done this, by working together within the organisation, dealing with external agents and being introduced to people by others.

You can extend your network in several ways:

- The simplest way is to collect business cards but remember to keep your filing system up to date because people move about.

- Be prepared to talk about yourself when attending meetings, conferences, exhibitions and similar events as a visitor. However, it is important in a conversation that you listen to the other person first before talking about yourself and what you can do. When attending events find who will be there and what they do so, if possible, you can arrange to meet specific people.

- Join networking groups and professional organisations like your local CIM branch and regularly attend meetings. Be positive about networking and actively seek out additional opportunities to make new contacts.

- When appropriate, wear your badge or name card so people can read it and keep a good stock of clean business cards with you when meeting new people. When giving one to a new contact, write something relevant on the back of the card to help them remember you, what you do and where you met.

- Engage in conversation with telephone contacts, visitors and colleagues in a friendly, helpful and professional way. Talk to as many people as you can within your organisation and externally.

- Read relevant journals and newspapers so you have an informed opinion about topical issues when conversing with new contacts.

Skills and attributes of the effective networker

If you are good at communicating with people and have developed the skills that have already been discussed then you have the potential to be an effective networker. There are a number of key success factors that you should also consider:

- Developing your interpersonal skills so you are a good listener and conversationalist.

- Being ready to talk about yourself, clearly and concisely.

- Building a reputation for reliability – if you have promised to get back to someone with information, make sure that it is done within the timescale agreed.
- Being aware of your personal appearance and body language.
- Maintaining a good record of contacts.
- Remembering and using people's names.
- Keeping up to date with current affairs and topical marketing issues.
- Developing a wide range of contacts.

Case Study – E-volution in relationships

The Head of Customer Services at West Minton College, Henry Price, was aware of the reduction in the number of informal face to face meetings taking place within the department and had noticed an increase in the number of emails he received. He decided to survey staff about their email usage and the benefits and disadvantages that increased usage might bring. The results were quite concerning.

Everyone was content with the system in that it enabled them to respond to customers and suppliers promptly, and they were not restricted to office hours. This was a particular benefit when dealing with overseas enquiries.

The speed at which information was available was seen as a definite benefit. However, most were complaining of information overload and receiving many communications that were not relevant to their job. Too many people were concerned that colleagues would fire off a message to start a discussion going when previously they would walk down the corridor and into the office to sort the problem out immediately.

There was also resentment by many people about the breach of confidentiality that was taking place. Some managers were using email to inform individuals of pay increases or to discuss personal problems. In one case, preparation for a disciplinary meeting had been made electronically without all communications being directed specifically to individuals involved.

One culture difference that was reported as an improvement by most was the opportunity for subordinates to communicate directly with senior managers. Before the widespread use of this form of communication, senior members of staff were protected by personal assistants who acted as gatekeepers.

However, the majority of people felt that the lack of real human interaction was a great disadvantage of email and it was suggested that the department's reputation for quality of service would suffer if it did not encourage live communication between people.

Questions

1. Communicating via email is seen as a major benefit for overseas customers. What are some of the uses that organisations might make of email to communicate with customers and clients?

2. What are the skills that might be lost if the use of email among staff rises at the expense of personal contact?

3. What are the potential disadvantages for organisations of using email to communicate with customers?

SUMMARY OF KEY POINTS

- People working in front-line roles are company representatives, so need to have skills that enable them to project the right image of the organisation in addition to carrying out their main tasks – appearance, body language, behaviour and telephone manner all contribute to the impression gained by visitors and others about the company.

- When dealing with visitors from overseas, marketers need to be aware of cultural differences and implications for looking after such visitors.

- Negotiation requires marketers to understand how to apply their interpersonal skills effectively when putting forward proposals and counter-arguments. The best outcome of negotiation is a win-win situation, which is much more likely if negotiators have prepared their cases well and are willing to listen to each other.

- Marketers require an understanding of the principles of entering into a contract and must get legal advice before agreeing to contractual obligations as these are absolute.

- Effective marketers develop a broad range of contacts that can help them in their work and hold a positive approach to networking.

Improving and developing own learning

The following projects are designed to help you to develop your knowledge and skills further by carrying out some research yourself. Feedback is not provided for this type of learning because there are no 'answers' to be found, but you may wish to discuss your findings with colleagues and fellow students.

Project A

At the next meeting you attend or when working with a group of people, observe the messages given by body language.

How easy is it to interpret non-verbal communication?

Did you look for clusters rather than single actions?

Also, consider the last few times that you made personal contact with an organisation as a customer or supplier.

How effective were front-line staff in identifying and meeting your requirements?

What were the differences between the different organisations?

What suggestions can you make for improvements?

You have probably completed a personal skills audit (Activity 2.1). Review this with regard to those skills that are important in relationship building.

What opportunities have you identified previously to develop these?

Have you considered on the job training or shadowing customer care staff, in your organisation or one you know well?

If possible ask a more experienced marketer to be a mentor to help you further build your confidence when dealing with visitors, more senior colleagues and external agents.

Project B

If you have not been involved in negotiations then ask to sit in with some more experienced marketers as they prepare to negotiate with suppliers or other external agents.

If you have taken part in negotiation then review the process discussed in this Session and identify what you would do differently next time.

Project C

Review your network of contacts and check currency.

When did you last speak to each one?

What else can you do to enlarge your network?

What skills do you most need to develop?

How can you do this?

Feedback on activities

Activity 2.1: Showing that you care

Your self-assessment checklist may include some or all of the following:

When dealing with customers do I:

	Always	Sometimes	Never
Make the customer feel special, greeting courteously and by name if possible?			
Use appropriate questions to find out specific requirements, seeking all relevant information?			

	Always	Sometimes	Never
Listen actively and respond immediately?			
Communicate clearly and pleasantly, avoiding unnecessary jargon?			
Deal with customer problems promptly and ensure satisfaction?			
Keep customers informed if there is an ongoing problem?			
Use my initiative to prevent customer dissatisfaction?			
Present barriers, or am I flexible and decisive to ensure customer needs are met and exceeded where possible?			
Ensure that the information I provide on products and services is clear and up to date?			
Pass on messages quickly and accurately to the right person and ensure that they are dealt with promptly?			
Create the right impression via my appearance and body language?			
Sell the benefits of the organisation's products and services?			
Reflect on how to improve the way that the organisation deals with customers and make positive suggestions to the right people?			

	Always	Sometimes	Never
Ensure that high standards of customer care are maintained at all times?			
Organise my own work so I can spend time with the customer?			

Activity 2.2: Ring, ring!

Good practice
- Smile.
- Be friendly but polite and helpful.
- Be prepared.
- Ask questions.
- Reflect back to clarify understanding.
- Take notes.
- Limit your talking.
- Do not jump to conclusions.
- Concentrate; don't be distracted.
- Don't interrupt.

How to minimise problems
- Answer promptly!
- Pass messages on quickly.
- Call back when promised – even if there is no news!
- Use callers' names.
- Don't keep people on hold for too long.
- Apologise if you have to leave the telephone to seek information.
- Explain what will happen next if passing to another department and let the next person know who is calling and why.
- Be patient.

Activity 2.3: Communicating with suppliers

[Headed stationery with The Shoppers Catalogue logo and address]

John Smith
Product Manager
ABC Ltd.
19 Lands End Road
Cardiff
Wales
CF3 7HG

14th September 2002

Dear John

I am delighted that you have decided to continue to advertise your products in our catalogue. As you know, we value loyalty and are very pleased to work with existing customers to agree a price that represents excellent value for money.

Following our conversation today, I have reviewed the figures we discussed and can confirm that the cost to ABC Ltd. of advertising in next year's Shopper's Catalogue will be £30 per insertion of up to 50 words using existing images.

Last year over 2 million catalogues were mailed to customers all over the UK and we anticipate a 10% increase in circulation next year. We have also invested in a new online version which is launched this week, thus increasing the opportunity to reach target groups and wider consumer groups.

I would like to take this opportunity to thank you for your business and will telephone you next week to discuss final details.

Yours sincerely

Chris Marsh
Marketing Manager

Activity 2.4: Frustration

i)   Possibly this is why it is useful to have a contingency plan.

ii) Cancelling at short notice is always a difficult situation to deal with, but for this and the above situation, the contract is likely to have protection clauses built in to deal with most circumstances that can be anticipated.

In the first case it is likely that the illness can be said to have frustrated the contract. However, in most cases, if cancelling supplies with short notice – even with good reason – the marketer must rely on the goodwill of the supplier and not frustration of contract to avoid paying for goods no longer required.

When planning, the marketer should always consider the worst case scenario and add contingency for this. For example, if sending invitations out to an outdoor event, give instructions for people attending should the event have to be moved elsewhere.

Session 3

Gathering information for marketing

Introduction

Marketers need information to help them make decisions. It is available from many sources both within and external to the organisation. Most organisations develop a Marketing Information System (MkIS) which is designed to provide the right people with the right information at the right time.

This Session explores the sources of data and information that can be used for secondary research and explains how to collate and analyse this information. In addition, it will consider how organisations gain intelligence about their competitors and how to gather information from overseas sources. The digital age has made information much more readily available but the downside of this is that many people are in danger of suffering overload. The intelligent marketer is the one who can source relevant data and use it appropriately to make effective decisions. This Session leads into the next Session that explores the use of marketing databases and others that explore the use of marketing and promotional activities.

LEARNING OUTCOMES

At the end of this Session you will be able to:

- Identify sources of information internally and externally to the organisation, including ICT-based sources such as Intranet and Internet.

- Explain information gathering techniques available

- Source and present information on competitor activities across the marketing mix.

- Investigate marketing and promotional opportunities using appropriate information gathering techniques.

- Gather information across borders.

What is data?

Data is the raw material collected by marketers when carrying out research. It is simply a collection of facts or figures such as the number of sales calls made by a salesperson each day or a list of product prices. It can be generated by the marketer through carrying out a survey (primary data) or collected via desk research from sources that already exist. This Session examines the gathering of secondary data, i.e. that which has already been published.

What is information?

Data that has been sorted and grouped together for a specific purpose is termed information. For example, when researching sales force efficiencies, if data is collected for each individual on the number of sales calls made per day and compared to data on the length of duration of each call and the geographic spread of customers, then inferences can be drawn about time and territory management. This information can be made available to others to help with planning calls or calculating manpower requirements.

The data referred to above should be available internally from records kept by the sales department but useful data and information for marketers also exists externally to the organisation. The limitations of both internal and external information is that it may not have been produced for the same purpose as the research that you are carrying out. Therefore, when doing secondary research it is often necessary to collect information from all relevant sources available to gain the specific information you require.

The marketing information system

All data and information used by marketers should be evaluated to determine validity – does it represent the true picture? – before being incorporated into the MkIS. Simple or routine decisions may be made on the basis of personal experience and judgement. However, where there are high risk factors then decision making must be well informed, based on reliable and valid information from both primary and secondary sources.

The MkIS is a system for collecting and storing information so it is readily available for people to use. Electronic systems and digital technology mean that huge amounts of information can be stored in a much smaller space than paper-based systems. Most organisations have a number of information systems that are linked electronically to improve accessibility across different functions. To ensure that commercially sensitive or confidential information is only available to the right person it will be password protected.

The analysis of information from different sources gives rise to marketing intelligence. For example, following a sales promotion, information might be analysed about the increase in sales during the promotion and compared to that of rival products and competitor activities as part of the evaluation process.

Activity 3.1: Information at your fingertips?

Review the different information storage and retrieval systems that your organisation uses.

How easy are they to use?

What improvements can you suggest?

Consider both paper-based systems and electronic systems and their relevant advantages and disadvantages.

Specific sources of information

As previously mentioned, secondary data and information is available within the organisation and outside.

Internal sources of information include:

Information source	Examples of data and information
Customer records and databases.	■ Customer records and databases. ■ Nature of purchase. ■ Frequency of purchase. ■ Value of purchase. ■ Volume of purchase. ■ Spending patterns. ■ Seasonal variations in product purchase. ■ Complaints and suggestions. ■ Results of customer satisfaction surveys.
PR and communications records and databases.	■ News releases. ■ Press cuttings. ■ Media interviews. ■ Evaluation of activities.

Information source	Examples of data and information
Research records and databases.	■ Published results of surveys and studies. ■ Trends and developments studies.
Sales records and databases.	■ Volume. ■ Prices and discounts. ■ Distribution. ■ Evaluation of results.
Promotions records.	■ Advertising activity and results. ■ Sales promotions and results. ■ Sponsorship activities.
Additional, including other functions of the organisation and company Intranet.	■ Accounts and finance records. ■ Production. ■ Special project evaluations. ■ Minutes of meetings. ■ Annual reports and communications to shareholders. ■ Informal sources such as the sales force and front-line staff.

External sources of information include:

Information source	Examples of data and information
Government statistics.	■ National and local statistics on changing demographics, regional, social trends etc.
Trade Associations.	■ Information on member organisations and contacts. ■ Reports and surveys on trends and development within the Industry.

Information source	Examples of data and information
Chamber of Commerce.	■ Information on member organisations and contacts. ■ Local business information. ■ Local trends and developments. ■ Export information.
Media.	■ Business news. ■ Market news. ■ Special reports and surveys on industries, marketing topics, companies and product trends and developments. ■ Marketing journals such as *Marketing, Marketing Business, Marketing Week* and *Campaign* – marketing news such as promotional activity, product launches, NPD, people in the news, advertising and special reports on marketing subjects.
Published market research.	■ Mintel Market Intelligence – consumer goods. ■ Keynote Reports – consumer goods, industry trends and developments.
Business directories.	■ Kompass – UK and Europe.
Libraries.	■ Reference section will hold census reports, journals, business and marketing directories and publications. ■ Most libraries have fully searchable online catalogues of papers and publications.

Information source	Examples of data and information
Internet – see also below.	■ Commercial organisations have a web site giving details on company history, background, recent news releases, annual report, information on product and services. ■ Press produce online publications with searchable archives. ■ Broadcast media publish business news with searchable archives. ■ All associations and publishers of directories, market research etc. produce information online about what is available.

Figure 3.1: Examples of internal and external secondary data sources

---

Activity 3.2: Collecting and storing information

There is a huge amount of marketing and business information available through commercial publications, libraries, government offices and other sources such as the Internet. As a marketer you should start to collect details of the sources of information that you might use and file them so they are available when required. Use a paper-based filing system or an electronic one; whichever allows best access for you at present.

An excellent table on sources of secondary data is given in the text book *Principles of Marketing* (3rd Edition), Brassington and Pettitt, published by Prentice-Hall. Look at Table 6.2 in Chapter 6: Marketing Information and Research. Where else will you find useful sources for secondary research?

Using the Internet to gather information

The Internet has opened up the range of information that is available to marketers, much of it free or on a pay-as-you-go-basis. Unless you know the address of the web site you wish to visit, you will need to use a search engine to find what you are looking for. Search engines such as Yahoo.com can be described as gateway sites on the Internet. The user simply accesses a site such as www.google.com or www.yahoo.com and types in key words or phrases to the search facility. The search engine then searches the web (memory) to find page listings that match the request. The pages are usually sorted by relevance, those being potentially the most useful presented first.

If visiting a site frequently it is useful to add it to your 'Favourites' which is a command on your web explorer toolbar. This means that you do not have to remember the site by name as it is now recorded on your system.

The amount of information that is readily available on competitors demonstrates two of the main advantages of the Internet – speed and accessibility. Examples of the type of information include:

- Product range and prices (online catalogues).

- Promotional activity.

- Company history and current strategies contained in annual reports.

- Competitor activities as reported in online journals and newspapers.

- Advertisements for salespeople on web sites – may indicate change in promotional focus such as increasing level of personal selling.

- Pending new product/service launches.

Activity 3.3: Power to consumers!

Go to the web site www.dti.gov.uk and research the Consumer Affairs Directorate. What are the:

i)   Aims of the CA Directorate?

ii)   Key Priorities of the CA Directorate?

Intranets

Many organisations have company Intranets. These employ the same technology as the Internet but are not available to users outside the company because they are protected by a firewall. Intranets are used as internal, interactive company communication channel for sending and storing messages, documents and information. Within the internal system access can be restricted as necessary so only authorised people can obtain certain categories of information.

The type of information that is available varies but most companies put business objectives and plans, company policies and procedures, catalogues, reports and plans that are used by different functions. The company newsletter and other marketing communications are also commonly circulated this way.

The development of company Intranets has made internal information readily accessible so the preparation of reports that draw information from a number of internal sources of information should be much easier. Also plans and reports can be circulated for comment; but security is essential if discussing commercially sensitive information.

Gathering information on competitors

Most organisations communicate freely with consumers, customers, suppliers, shareholders and the media. The information that they generate includes newsletters, annual reports, promotional literature, advertising and news releases.

Therefore if needing to gather information about competitors you will find that there is a lot of it about! The reasons companies check what rival organisations are doing include:

- To identify the strengths and weaknesses of major competitors.

- To monitor the market segments that rival organisations are targeting to help inform own targeting decisions.

- To identify current level of competitor activity such as sales promotions, advertising etc. that might impact on own promotional activity.

- To identify competitor pricing strategies to compare with own.

- To monitor changes in levels of competitor activity during product life cycles.

- To identify new entrants to the market – and those that are leaving, particularly during the growth phase of the life cycle.

- To help predict future competitor activity by analysing previous patterns etc.

- To identify new ways of reaching customers – most organisations learnt a lot from those who were early entrants into the e-shopping market and used it to avoid making the same mistakes. In a new market there is relatively little information available so it is very important to monitor and analyse competitor success and failure.

- To watch the development of new or modified products that might attract sales from own products.

- To help make strategic, operational and tactical decisions about what to do in the future.

All competitor activities are potential threats so it is essential that environmental scanning and analysis of rival products and organisations is undertaken on a regular basis. The key to success is in proactivity – identifying what is happening in time to make plans to respond rather than being reactive and risking being taken by surprise. It is widely acknowledged that product life cycles are being reduced due to the speed at which information becomes available and the rate of technological advance. Therefore, competitive advantage is difficult to sustain so all threats need to be identified and dealt with as early as possible.

Activity 3.4: What are your competitors up to?

You have been asked to carry out some desk research into the recent activities of several main competitors.

List some of the sources of information that you might use.

Ask other students and other marketing contacts for their ideas to help you build a comprehensive list.

You may wish to use this information to compile a report on the competitors for one of your products and services.

Presenting and interpreting numerical information

Graphs and charts are commonly used to present numerical data and can be very effective, as long as the appropriate format is used.

Pie charts are probably the simplest and one of the commonest used to show the relative size of the different elements that make up the total. Look at the following pie chart showing the monthly sales of four major products sold by one company.

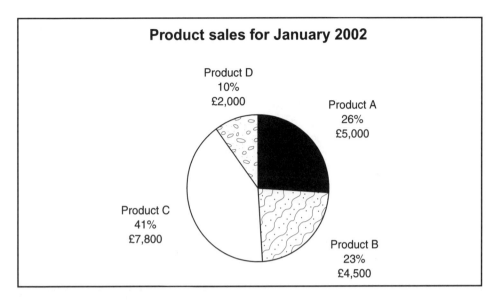

Figure 3.2: Example of pie chart

Displaying percentages and absolute values on the pie chart makes it easy to see and compare the relative contributions made by each product in addition to the monetary value of sales. It provides information to help make decisions about employment of resources. If all else were equal, then resources could be apportioned according to the percentage contribution, so Product C attracts the highest percentage of resources available. However, the real situation is much more complex with lots of variables needing to be taken into account. For example, Product C might be at the mature stage in its life cycle requiring little promotion because customers are loyal and there are few rival products allowing resources to be used elsewhere. So, a chart like this is only as good as the data on which it is based.

If showing quarterly sales of the same four products then a bar chart might be used. This readily displays comparison values making it very easy to spot trends and track progress. Bar charts can be displayed horizontally or vertically as in the following example.

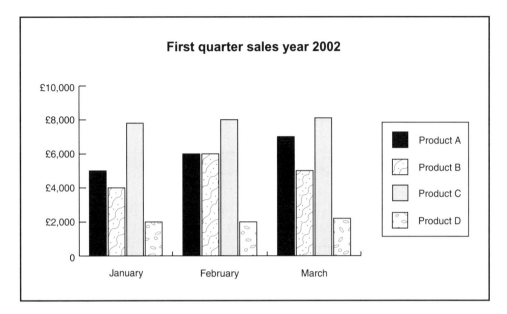

Figure 3.3: Example of bar chart

From the information in Figure 3.3 it is easy to track what has happened to sales of the individual products over the first quarter. Sales for Products C and D have remained relatively static compared to Products A and B. However, although there has been a continued upward trend for Product A, sales of Product B have fluctuated although the overall trend is up.

The bar chart makes it easy to summarise related data.

Another commonly used graph is the line graph or multiple line graph where more than one line is used.

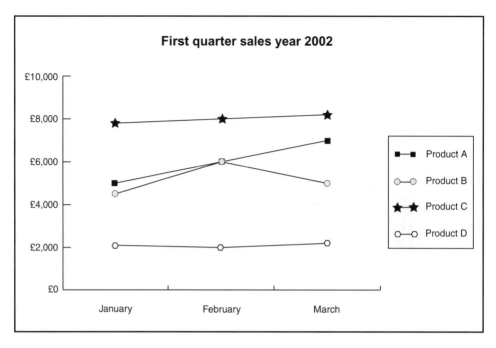

Figure 3.4: Example of a line graph

When presenting any information as a diagram, picture or chart, simplicity is essential to help the viewer interpret the information. From Figure 3.4, it can be seen that more than four lines on one graph would cause confusion as it becomes difficult to follow individual lines – especially if they are not spaced out as in the example shown above.

Activity 3.5: Presenting information

A colleague has carried out some international research into usage of the Internet by small companies (less than 100 employees) in the food and drink industry. The following table shows some of the findings. The first column lists what percentage of companies in each country use the Internet to identify suppliers and the second the percentage that actually order online whenever possible.

Look at how the information is presented and answer the questions set out below.

Country	Identify suppliers	Order online
USA	63%	41%
Britain	54%	40%
Germany	54%	45%
France	52%	26%
Sweden	31%	14%
Norway	19%	11%

Questions

1. What are the benefits of using percentages rather than numbers when presenting this information?

2. What are the benefits of presenting numerical information in a table rather than text?

3. In what other format might the information be presented?

Gathering information from overseas

Information from overseas may be in a different language to your native language so will require translation. There are several problems that might arise:

- Translation – an article written in one language cannot be translated word for word into another language because sentence structure and phrasing is different.

- Vocabulary – words have different meanings in different languages. This is not a major problem but one that might cause confusion.

- Equivalent sources – it is unlikely that national business directories, organisations publishing survey reports and government sources of information will be in a common format. Therefore, equivalent information might not be available for comparisons etc. There are many more international business directories and information services than there used to be, due to the global nature of trading, so it is likely than this problem will continue to decrease.

- Access to the Internet has made it much easier for marketers to gather information on overseas competitors and markets.

Case Study – Centrica

Centrica has undergone transformation organisationally and culturally and in a relatively short space of time. When British Gas was privatised in 1997, Centrica was a product of the de-merger, along with the BG Group.

As part of the deal Centrica was given the right to the British Gas brand, which now also covers other home services such as electricity and security as well as gas. It has launched Goldfish, an organically-grown financial services brand and last year it bought the Automobile Association. That amounts to an astonishing 20 million households on the books, which is set to rise with a new telecoms service about to be launched.

Simon Waugh, Director of Marketing, realises how particularly unsettling the pace of change has been for those on the front-line who are finding the way they used to operate turned upside down. The staff are now expected to be prompt, productive, customer-focused and act as ambassadors of the brand in every customer contact. This, as anyone who has had frustrating experiences with service calls will attest, is quite a hurdle to climb.

He acknowledges this but insists the company is getting better: "If I said we're there – well we're not. The point is that you can never programme human beings to think the same way. Some love the changes, others haven't wanted to be part of the new dynamic and have left. Its not about age, but attitude."

Spending a day out in the field every three months, whether in an engineer's van, a call centre or on an AA patrol, helps senior management see the reality at the sharp end. And they are trying to exploit what can be a rich source of customer feedback – the complaints. In many companies complaints are aggregated, homogenised and sanitised by the time they reach head office. For the last

18 months at Centrica, at the instigation of Chief Executive, Roy Gardner, Simon Waugh and his counterparts heading the other business divisions have been meeting monthly, not only to investigate the top reasons for complaints but to try to do something about them.

Source: *Marketing Business*, September 2000.

Questions

1. How has information been used to improve services at Centrica?

2. What other information would help Simon Waugh and Centrica develop a competitive edge on customer service?

3. What are the potential benefits for working relationships of Centrica's policy of encouraging senior managers to spend time in the field on a regular basis?

SUMMARY OF KEY POINTS

■ Marketers need reliable and valid data and information to make informed decisions.

■ There are many sources of secondary data including government statistics and records, marketing and market research reports, business directories and the Internet, so marketers need to know how to access these.

■ The Internet can enable the marketer to find out information about competitors and their activities from online brochures and prices, company web sites and business web sites including the marketing press and main newspapers online.

■ When collecting information from overseas the marketer might find that equivalent sources are not available and that the information is not translated into his/her native language.

■ Marketing Information Systems should enable the right people to access the right information at the right time.

- Presenting information in the right format enhances interpretation – where possible, financial information should be presented as a table, graph or chart.

Improving and developing own learning

The following projects are designed to help you to develop your knowledge and skills further by carrying out some research yourself. Feedback is not provided for this type of learning because there are no 'answers' to be found, but you may wish to discuss your findings with colleagues and fellow students.

Project A

Go to the web sites of the:

i)   Financial Times newspaper www.ft.com and click on Industries. Review the contents and read any articles that are relevant to you and your organisation. Also research the Special Reports and FT Surveys that are published on this site to discover those which are useful to you as a marketer.

ii)   British Broadcasting Corporation www.bbc.co.uk and click on BBC News. Use the search facility to look for articles on e-commerce.

Project B

Conduct some secondary research into a market that interests you. This may be connected to a recreational interest (adventure holidays) or a market that you know well (fast food, fashion, soft drinks, healthcare, financial services etc.).

Try to find out:

i)   Size of the market.

ii)   Recent developments and trends.

iii)   Major 'players' – producers etc.

iv)   Market structure – products and services available, who the buyers are, methods of distribution, etc.

v)   Characteristics of buyers/customer profiles

Project C

Visit the web site of your own organisation, or one you know well, and read the annual report.

What information might this provide to rival companies on current performance, strategies and future intentions?

Feedback on activities

Activity 3.1: Information at your fingertips?

Your answer will depend on the different systems that you reviewed. You may have thought of:

- Electronic and paper-based information systems used by your organisation – for example what information is available to you via your company Intranet?

- Internet – how many different search engines do you use?

- CD-ROM.

- Personal organiser – do you use an electronic organiser or a paper-based diary? How quickly can you check appointments on your system if someone asks you to change a date?

- Address book.

- Library – a rich source of data and information that is indexed.

The suggestions for improvement might be based on:

- The need to carry less paper around with you.

- A requirement for a faster system and one that allows you to cross-reference more easily.

- Space – does your information take up too much of it?

- Ability to find what you are looking for more readily.

Activity 3.2: Collecting and storing information

Remember to update your information and review your filing system on a regular basis to ensure your methods of recording and storing information are efficient and effective. Your indexing system should allow you to find the information you require easily without searching through everything that you have stored!

To add to your information:

- Consult other students, your tutors and marketing network of contacts.
- Refer to other text books.
- Note interesting web sites and look at those they provide links to.
- Look at the range of journals, newspapers, research reports, publications and directories available at libraries.
- Explore the CIM web site.

Activity 3.3: Power to consumers!

i) The aims of the DTI's CA Directorate are to help consumers make well-informed purchases and protect them from unsafe products and unfair business practices. The mission is to help all consumers get a fair deal.

ii) Key priorities include:

- Improving advice and information available to consumers.
- Modernising consumer institutions.
- Updating relevant laws and regulation that provide protection for consumers.
- Improving enforcement of the above.
- Enhancing consumer safety.
- Promoting consumer interests.

Activity 3.4: What are your competitors up to?

Relevant sources might include:

- Published Directories such as *Kompass and Key British Enterprises* (KBE).
- Internet – most companies publish annual reports, catalogues and other information on their web site.

- Newspapers and industry journals or trade press – often also available as online versions.

- Online databases such as Reuters Textline which contains information on companies and industries within articles from worldwide press and trade journals.

- Journals such as *Marketing*, *Marketing Week* and *Campaign* provide up to date information about competitors' promotional activities and other news such as new product launches and predictions.

- Company sales force can be a rich source of information about competitors – as can all front-line staff because people will pass on information to them in the course of conversation.

- Competitors themselves – use the telephone to make up to the minute enquiries about prices, product availability and current promotions.

- Your personal contacts might be able to direct you to additional material that has been published; so much information is available today that it is impossible to keep track of everything you might need to know about, so tap into other people's knowledge.

Activity 3.5: Presenting information

1. Using percentages rather than numbers when presenting numerical information makes it easier to analyse and compare the results from different countries. For example, by grouping the data from the highest to the lowest it can be immediately seen that in 4 of the 6 countries studied, over 50% of the companies taking part in the survey use the Internet to identify suppliers. It can also be seen that the same 4 countries also show the highest percentage of companies using online ordering facilities, although in France this is significantly lower than in the other three countries. This leads researchers to ask further questions as to why this might be.

2. The benefits of presenting numerical information in a table rather than as descriptive text should now be obvious. It makes it much easier to analyse – to compare and contrast the data and draw implication that can then be tested out or compared with information from other sources.

3. The information might also be presented as a chart:

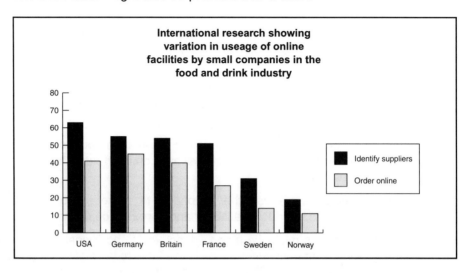

Session 4

Marketing databases

Introduction

Marketers need information to plan activities and target effectively. Customer databases are used to help identify groups or market segments for specific marketing activities such as sales promotions. This Session explores how marketing databases are organised, used and maintained. It also informs marketers of the main guidelines laid down by the Data Protection Act 1998.

LEARNING OUTCOMES

At the end of this Session you will be able to:

- Maintain a customer database, information collection and usage.

- Investigate customers via the database and develop bases for segmentation.

- Discuss how to identify marketing and promotional opportunities.

Why segment markets?

Market segmentation is the process whereby a larger market is broken down into smaller groups that have similar characteristics and buying requirements. This makes it easier for organisations to identify different opportunities and smaller companies may be able to find a niche or opportunity that is not satisfied by larger ones. An example of the latter is the consumer market for healthy, organic foods that is served by smaller, specialist companies.

The opposite of segmentation is a market where each buyer has individual requirements, so only those who are to offer bespoke products and services will be successful. This is more usual in business to business markets where a customised piece of equipment is required to meet a specific requirement. For example, a utility company building a small pumping station might need a custom-designed electrical control panel.

An organisation carries out market research in order to understand the structure of that market. That information can be used to identify how to segment the market. For example, segments may be identified according to lifestyle (convenience foods, health foods, low calorie foods) or level of spend (chain store label, budget, designer clothes). Criteria for segmenting markets is discussed in greater detail later in the Session.

When organisations have been able to identify clearly different customer segments with specific product requirements it is much easier for them to understand how to meet those needs. By closely monitoring what is happening in a defined segment the organisation can also spot changing requirements and respond effectively.

Therefore, when operating in a segmented market, organisations gain knowledge and understanding of their customers, so are able to target markets that other competitors may not be able to reach. By deploying resources where there is potential for the greatest advantage, organisations are operating more efficiently. They may develop product features that rivals may find difficult to copy or streamline processes to reduce costs to enable them to become cost leaders. However, it is clear that organisations are not able to do this unless they become skilled at gathering and using marketing and market information.

Activity 4.1: As you like it!

As the Marketing Manager for a health club offering pool, sauna and steam rooms, gym, squash and health and beauty services you are listing different target audience groups in order to identify different categories of membership such as individual and family membership.

Make some notes in preparation for a meeting with other club managers.

Present your information in a table.

Methods of segmenting markets

There are many different ways to group buyers in a market. The key defining factors are the product and the relevant characteristics of the buyers. For example, the car market might be segmented according to socio-economic factors such as income, social class and occupation. However, if buying washing powder different individuals will be looking for different features and benefits such as an environmentally friendly product, whiteness or suitability for delicate fabrics.

Some of the commonest criteria used for market segmentation are identified below:

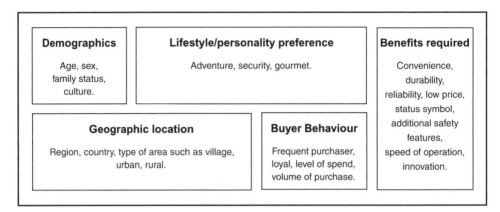

Figure 4.1: Criteria for segmenting markets

It can be appreciated from the above that it is much easier for marketers to target customers accurately if they operate in a segmented market. For example, one holiday company might specialise in activity holidays, whereas Saga targets those over fifty years of age. Each group has different characteristics and requirements so will respond to different marketing activities. Over time marketers can become very knowledgeable about what their customers want and how to communicate with them if they gather and analyse data about previous marketing successes and failures.

It is possible to use the same criteria for segmenting both consumer and business markets. However, in the latter the buying decision is often more complex and may involve a number of people. Therefore, additional criteria might include new purchase or re-buy, product type and degree of customisation and the stage at which the purchase decision is at – for example, interested or awaiting final decision – so resources (salespeople) can be deployed appropriately.

Homogeneous and heterogeneous markets

Segmented markets exist between these two extremes. In *homogeneous* markets buyers all have the same needs. They may be seeking raw materials for a manufacturing process such as waste paper to make recycled paper or chemical to manufacture fertilisers.

At the other end of the scale is the *heterogeneous* market where buyers all have different needs. This is common in the business to business markets where one large organisation might represent the market. Major airlines might be individual markets for manufacturers of large passenger carriers such as the Airbus A380. The business relationships in such markets are long term and may start from the early stages of product development, through to testing of prototypes and beyond product launch.

Marketing databases

Marketers need to collect data on customers and their buying habits in order to help them identify opportunities for future promotions and other marketing activities. For example, opticians and dentists send patients reminders when their next eye examination or check-up is due. Opticians also send out direct mailings to tell customers about special offers such as free prescription sunglasses with each purchase of spectacles over a certain value.

In order to do this they need a means of storing the data and the ability to manage it – a software programme. Such systems are termed marketing databases. They enable the marketer to:

- Store customer data such as name, address, frequency of purchase, date of last purchase, amount of last purchase.

- Search for specific information such as customers who made a purchase between 18 months and 2 years ago and who spent over £100.

- Identify the number of customers who are in each defined target group – for example, if the above search was refined to customers who spent between £100 and £150 then there would be fewer in the group. This might be done if the original search identified a group that was too large for budget purposes. Alternatively the search may be widened if the group is too small.

Each piece of data that is required is entered into a field – a column in the database. Fields can take numerical data or text or combination such as street name and number of house, e.g. 50 Newmarket Avenue. Complete customer addresses are normally entered into several fields so searches can be carried out by district, city and post or zip code.

Organisations can purchase database software 'off the shelf' or have a bespoke database built for them. Database architecture is the term used to describe how the database is constructed. Most today are 'relational' databases that can be described as a series of linked or related tables of data rather than a series of records which the older common architecture used (sequential files).

The cost of using sequential files is much lower than a relational database but it produces an inflexible system that will have limited use. The fields to be searched must be specified in advance because changes cannot be easily made at a later date.

Therefore, the marketer needs to be able to predict future requirements accurately. However, since the cost of construction is relatively low, this type of database might be appropriate for standard queries.

Relational databases are constructed so that data from different sections or tables can be joined or combined to answer queries put in by the end user. Hence the name relational – all types of data can be related so the potential nature of searches does not have to be determined before the database is built.

At the front end of a database there is usually a user-friendly piece of software that allows entry of queries. One of the most common languages in use is SQL – Structured Query Language. This is menu driven so the user needs only to know what commands are possible rather than having to understand the architecture of the database itself or the intricacies of the language.

Activity 4.2: Questions about customers

Knowing that you are undertaking a marketing course, your manager has asked you to contribute to the process of constructing a new customer database.

Write a checklist (in the form of questions) to help consider the type of information that will be required.

Customer database applications

The type of data stored will depend on what it will be used for. Customer databases are used extensively in both business to business and consumer markets. Applications vary but a major use for the tactical marketer is to enhance targeting. Therefore, in the consumer market useful data includes customer identification, purchases made, frequency, volume, value and other distinguishing features or relevant preferences. For example, Amazon.com record the type of genre that customers enjoy reading and suggest other titles that they might also enjoy. In the business to business market, data is stored about individual organisations, the business they are in, size, purchase details, contact names and job titles and credit rating etc.

Most people are familiar with the most common type of application, direct marketing. Knowing the past history of purchases and spending patterns enables marketers to target customers with the right product and/or promotion at the right time. This might be to encourage a replacement purchase, such as a new car or an example of cross selling or up selling. A wine merchant might target groups of wine drinkers with special offers on champagne just before Christmas or collaborate with a holiday company to offer reduced rates on holidays to French wine making regions to include tours of vineyards producing the type of wine they enjoy drinking.

The data can also be used to help organisations identify their best customers and target resources into their most profitable areas. A salesman might regularly call on a business to check that products are still giving satisfaction and discuss future requirements. Loyal customers might be offered additional discounts or benefits such as corporate hospitality at marketing events.

Customer databases are often used for loyalty programmes. Customers who regularly buy a premium or branded product may receive regular newsletters with further promotions, news about the product and its parent company or they might be invited to join an exclusive club. This is designed to make customers become part of the brand experience and prevent them from looking for substitutes. Many of these communications and direct mailings are personalised to encourage people to feel that they are being written to as an individual, not as part of a mass marketing campaign.

Activity 4.3: Junk mail annoys consumers

Read the article taken from *Marketing Business*, September 2001 and answer the questions set:

Marketers are vastly underestimating the level of annoyance consumers experience when receiving unsolicited direct mail. The only communication that annoys them slightly more is intrusive telephone calls, according to a recent survey conducted by technology company Bell & Howell.

The survey suggests that there is also a discrepancy between consumer reaction to unsolicited marketing and marketers' views on what that reaction would be. Marketers gave unsolicited post a relatively low irritation score of 51% but consumers report a far higher annoyance level of 80%. Both groups concur that uninvited telephone calls are the most annoying unsolicited communication, ranked at 90% by marketers and 82% by consumers.

The surprisingly strong consumer reaction to unsolicited direct mail suggests that the much-heralded techniques of targeting and one-to-one communication are far from being appreciated by consumers.

Over the next few years, marketers are expecting a dramatic rise in the use of email as a communication channel. Currently 9% of all direct marketing campaigns are sent by email, yet by 2003 that figure is predicted to rise to 27%. Despite this anticipated rise in direct email campaigns, marketers do not believe direct mail volumes will be adversely affected, predicting a 7% rise in volumes during the same period.

If email marketing does accelerate marketers will need to be careful about targeting messages to interested recipients only. Research by communication consultancy, Rogan has found that the use of email in the UK has grown by some 74% in the last year. It now takes executives around two hours a day to sort through their messages, 35% of which are irrelevant to their job.

Questions

1. How well does the survey results suggest that marketers understand the tolerance levels of consumers to direct mail and unsolicited phone calls?

2. Why should marketers be cautious about assuming consumers will welcome direct marketing via email?

3. What reasons can you suggest for the comment that marketers do not expect the volume of direct mail to be adversely affected despite the rise in the use of email as a communication channel?

Maintenance of customer databases

In addition to keeping the database updated – adding new customers or organisations, updating existing entries and removing those that are inactive – there are a number of maintenance tasks that should be carried out on a regular basis.

Many databases contain a significant number of duplicated entries due to a name being spelt incorrectly so a new customer is created. This not only wastes valuable marketing resources but also risks annoying the customer who received two mailings at the same time. That person is not likely to be impressed with the organisation on receiving information with an incorrect name or address.

Keeping the database up to date, through responding to customer requests and mail returns, is a key issues for database managers. If mail is returned marked 'receiver gone away', or relatives contact an organisation to let them know a customer is deceased, then the database should be amended immediately as further mailings will cause upset.

The database should also be secure so information is only available to authorised people for specific purposes – this is discussed in the next section on data protection. In addition, the organisation needs to ensure that back-up systems are in place should their primary system fail.

In business to business markets it is important to realise that contacts change as they move departments, are promoted or leave the organisation. This might represent a new opportunity elsewhere but it also means that it is worth developing close relationships with key accounts so they keep you updated on any changes in personnel or requirements.

Data protection act 1998

The Data Protection Act came into force on 1st March 2000, replacing an earlier Act, and now applies to some paper records as well as personal information held on computers. Full information is available on the Department of Trade and Industry web site – www.dataprotection.gov.uk. This new Act reflects the European Union's increasing emphasis on an individual's right to privacy and the protection of their data. It requires businesses to further consider how they protect personal data that they store and gives more rights to individuals to access that data.

The Act covers rules for:

- Information handling – data must be fairly and lawfully processed, secure, accurate, adequate for purpose (strictly limited) and not excessive and not be kept for longer than is necessary.

- Processing – strictly controlled, and data subjects must be told the identity of the data controller and why that information is to be processed. In addition, individuals must give their consent.

- Sensitivity of data – sensitive personal data may only be processed under strict conditions including employment purposes and administration of justice or legal proceedings. Sensitive data includes political opinions, racial or ethnic origin, religious beliefs, health etc.

- Transfer of personal data outside the EEA (which includes Norway, Iceland and Liechtenstein in addition to the 15 EU member states) – "Personal data may only be transferred to third countries if those countries ensure an adequate level of protection for the rights and freedoms of data subjects".

- Rights of access for individuals – data subjects have right of access to see what data is held about themselves and can apply to the Court to order an amendment or destruction if details are inaccurate. They also have an absolute right to prevent direct marketing to them by requesting that a data controller does not process data relating to them for this purpose.

The increased rights of individuals mean that organisations need to keep records of people who have served notices on them regarding the holding and processing of their personal data. This has major implications for marketers who must ensure that their activities and communications comply with the requirements of the Act. There are already regulations in place whereby individuals can prevent direct marketing to them – the Telecommunications Regulations (Data Protection and Privacy) which give individuals the right to withhold their consent for unsolicited telecommunications such as telephone calls and faxes.

Activity 4.4: Data protection act 1998

Visit www.dataprotection.gov.uk and write down the eight enforceable principles of good practice that anyone processing personal data must comply with.

Read the full explanations of the eight principles.

Consider what implications they have for the way your organisation is using personal data.

Case Study – Net benefits

The UK student population numbers around 2 million and is a media-savvy group representing a diverse market, but one that includes some with a relatively high disposable income. The downside is that students are hard to profile accurately. While there are the obvious common denominators of age and occupation, defining students beyond this becomes more difficult. An Oxbridge art history student may not have much in common with someone studying hairdressing in Kirkcaldy, Scotland. Also, what about the mature, part-time student!

In addition, media tastes are diverse. The *Guardian*-reading stereotype may once have existed, but today a media buyer looking to reach students would be hard pressed to draw up a watertight strategy. As mass-market TV steadily gives way to numerous cable and satellite offers, the problem of reaching the undergraduate population becomes even harder. Against this backdrop the rise of the Internet looks like a marketer's dream. Originally a university-based facility, the Internet has exceptionally high penetration among UK students and has become integrated into their lifestyles both on and off campus. If one medium is guaranteed to reach the student audience, this is it.

However, for many consumers, the novelty of cyberspace has not taken long to wear off. Technological innovation has had to work hard to keep up with expectations. Students in particular have a broad experience of the Internet and are adept at recognising cutting-edge technology and dismissing anything that appears old-fashioned.

In the time it takes to develop and launch a web site, the ideas within it can already have become passé. Text has given way to images, animation, video, web-cams and sound: simple information has been superseded by chat-rooms, e-zines and e-commerce. It seems as if the empty vessel of the Internet is filling up rapidly with the sophistication of traditional marketing.

But the Internet also works some strange alchemy, which distorts even modern marketing rules. Speed and interactivity have become critical. Compared to other media such as TV and radio, the Internet engenders short attention spans and a dislike of passivity.

So how can a hard-to-define consumer group be reached by a hard-to-use medium? How about lifestyle sites? Lifestyle sites are a hybrid of magazine and private member's club. Through a mix of entertainment and information combined with careful branding, these sites are not just vehicles for brands, they are brands in their own right, and therefore have value in the consumer's eyes. Hard sell e-tailing brands are inappropriate for many brands, which instead need to opt for building up awareness, credibility and eventually loyalty.

A good example is Marmite, which linked up with hot-toast.com through sponsorship of the regular opinion poll and appears on the homepage in its familiar packaging. It neatly side-steps one of the own-goals of Internet marketing – the banner ad – which is causing increasing frustration and annoyance to browsers. Poor targeting, uncreative execution and haphazard locations have meant that they have become an online 'sheep dip' which most people prefer to avoid.

Marmite is the only brand to appear on the homepage which is unusual. Many surfers will tell you that there is nothing worse than a homepage that is a mish-mash of buttons, banners and brand names, yet site owners persist in perpetuating this. Consumers are turned off by the hard sell approach and none more so than young people.

For the lifestyle site, content is king. Success depends on a continual race to incorporate new elements and techniques. Pages need to download quickly and sites need to evolve constantly and improve. The mainstay of news, sports and weather has quickly been overtaken by chat-rooms, agony aunts and celebrity interviews.

Hot-toast.com has all the usual features expected by users with content provided by appropriate 'youth' sources. News and sport is provided by various partners. Interviews focus on cult celebrities which the target audience grew up with. In addition, Stepstone, the online recruitment agency, provides users with one of the most comprehensive graduate appointment databases in existence.

Getting under the radar of students will never be easy but it is clear that the commitment to reach this group continues to grow. Student lifestyle sites will continue to define themselves with increasing clarity. While some may fail, a few central players will remain, effectively creating a 'cyberspace' market sector. For brand owners seeking to woo a student audience, early involvement will quickly show an impressive payback – the only caveat will be 'don't take too long to think about it'.

Source: Adapted from an article in *Marketing Business*, April 2000.

Questions

1. Why do lifestyle sites represent an ideal route to the student market?

2. How can information on customer preferences be collected via the Internet?

3. What are the lessons that other site owners can learn from hot-toast.com's approach to site design and content?

SUMMARY OF KEY POINTS

- Markets are segmented to aid accurate targeting.

- Markets can be segmented using many different criteria including age, geographical location and frequency of product use.

- Organisations create customer databases to store data on customer profiles, purchase decisions, preferences etc.

- Sophisticated database technology means that marketers can identify specific groups of customers and use this information to target more accurately.

- The Data Protection Act 1998 has tightened up on the way organisations can store and use personal data, so marketers need to be aware of the legal implications of using personal data.

Improving and developing own learning

The following projects are designed to help you to develop your knowledge and skills further by carrying out some research yourself. Feedback is not provided for this type of learning because there are no 'answers' to be found, but you may wish to discuss your findings with colleagues and fellow students.

Project A

Consider organisations that operate in segmented markets such as holiday companies and car manufacturers.

What are the criteria used for segmenting each?

Within each segment what are the characteristics of each group?

How would you promote products and services to each target group?

You might like to do this as a group activity with other students or colleagues. Do this for you own organisation if appropriate.

Project B

Visit www.theidm.com, the web site of the Institute of Direct Marketing, and review their online enquiry form.

How effective is it compared to others that you have seen?

Do you think it encourages the right people to respond?

Is it easy to complete?

Are sufficient options offered?

Also, consider the direct mailings that you receive. How well targeted are they?

How many do you respond to?

Would you be more or less likely to respond to email?

How does this compare with unsolicited telephone calls?

Compare your feelings with those of others in your family.

Project C

Organisations like Amazon.com use databases for to store information on stock that customers can search.

Visit www.amazon.com and search the database for books on marketing to see how quickly the information is made available to you.

Feedback on activities

Activity 4.1: As you like it!

You may have thought of some of the following – and different categories according to the limits of your imagination!

Membership type	User characteristics
Full Individual – All facilities at all times.	People who want to be able to use all facilities at any time including weekdays (perhaps during lunch hours), weekends and evenings.
Off-peak Individual – All facilities during weekdays 9am to 5pm and some time during the weekends to be decided (e.g. after 4pm on Saturday and Sundays?)	Those who are able to come regularly during weekdays from 9am to 5pm when many other members are at work. May include shift workers, parents with children at school (to increase usage consider offering crèche facilities?), retired people, self-employed, working from home.
Full Family – All facilities at all times.	Up to 2 parents and 2 children with a supplementary fee for each additional child. For families who want to be able to use all facilities as individuals or as a family at any time including weekdays, weekends and evenings.

Membership type	User characteristics
Off-peak Family – All facilities during weekdays 9am to 5pm and some time during the weekends to be decided (e.g. after 4pm on Saturday and Sundays?)	Up to 2 parents and 2 children with a supplementary fee for each additional child. For families who want to come during off-peak times – may include shift workers with older children at college who have free time during the day or parents with pre-school children who want to come when it is quieter during the day. May offer the option to upgrade during school holidays?
Temporary/Monthly Full or Off-peak.	For people who work away from home for significant periods at a time or those who have work fluctuating commitments. May also work as a taster and perhaps an incentive can be offered, such as a discount on the first year's membership for those who want to 'try before they buy'.
Concessions.	Reduced fees for OAPs, students, unemployed?

Activity 4.2: Questions about customers

- Who are our customers?
- What do they want?
- What do they buy?
- Where do they come from?
- Why do they come to us?
- When do they buy?
- How often do they buy?
- How much do they spend?

Activity 4.3: Junk mail annoys consumers

1. Marketers appear to be vastly underestimating the level of consumer annoyance to direct mail. They gave it a relatively low irritation score of 51% whereas consumers were obviously much more annoyed by this form of marketing, giving it a much higher irritation score of 80%. Consumers were

slightly more irritated by unsolicited telephone calls ranking it at 82% which was not unexpected by marketers who thought that their irritation factor would be even higher. The survey suggests that marketers are mistaken if they think that consumers are not as annoyed by unsolicited mail as unsolicited telephone calls. The irritation factors are high and remarkably close.

2. Although many more people are using email the signs are that they may be overwhelmed by the level of traffic. Research suggests that executives are taking around 2 hours to sort through messages of which 35% are not relevant to their work. It is unlikely that they would welcome more messages that have no direct relationship to their job. Even if the email is accurately targeted, can marketers assume that consumers will be tolerant of unsolicited emails than they are of unsolicited mail and telephone calls?

3. Although email is less expensive than direct mail this method is still likely to be used as not everyone uses the Internet. Post is still most likely to get through – many consumers do not have an email address (and this varies in different age groups) and may be out when the telephone rings or not have a direct line. Everyone receives mail so it is still the communication channel that is common to everyone.

Activity 4.4: Data protection act 1998

The eight principles say that data must be:

■ Fairly and lawfully processed.
■ Processed for limited purposes.
■ Adequate, relevant and not excessive.
■ Accurate.
■ Not kept longer than necessary.
■ Processed in accordance with the data subject's rights.
■ Secure.
■ Not transferred to countries without adequate protection.

You should have considered the way your organisation collects, stores, protects and uses personal information and the rights of access it provides to data subjects.

Session 5

Planning tools for organising events

Introduction

This Session is about organising effective marketing activities so it examines the type of events that you might be called upon to organise and provides some relevant planning tools and techniques. Most marketers are aware of the need to set clear objectives and schedule activities so deadlines are met, but are not as good at evaluating effectiveness following the event. Evaluating results will be referred to here but covered in more detail in the next Session.

Venues are an important part of the success of events so criteria for selection are considered, as are budgets! Working to a budget can be difficult because it is not always easy to predict exact costs. The implications for budget are explored but you will also find Sessions 11 and 12 helpful in this respect.

LEARNING OUTCOMES

At the end of this Session you will be able to:

- Demonstrate an awareness of successful applications of marketing across a variety of sectors and sizes of business.

- Explain how marketing makes use of planning techniques: objective setting: co-ordinating, measuring results and evaluating results to support the organisation.

- Appraise and select a venue based on given criteria and make appropriate recommendations.

Different types of marketing activities

The range of marketing events is enormous so it is impossible to cover them all in this Session. You may have been involved in organising some already, so you will know that examples include:

- Conferences which may be large international events or the quarterly in-house sales conference.

- Press conferences to communicate important news to journalists and press representatives.

- The opening of a new outlet such as a new retail branch in a shopping mall.

- Outdoor shows such as agricultural and horticultural events, for example the annual Chelsea Flower Show.

- Meetings such as the annual shareholder's meeting.

- Seminars where eminent academics come together to discuss the latest research and opinions.

- Consumer exhibitions such as the annual London Boat Show where the general public can browse the latest products and services available for the boating and sailing enthusiast.

- Business to business exhibitions, also referred to as Trade Shows, are exactly what the name suggests. They attract specific media interest because they are specific to one industry such as holiday and leisure or the water industry. Publicity is vital to the success of exhibiting at this type of show due to the intensity of competition – the more visual and memorable the better.

It is important to note that organisations need to consider very carefully the most cost-effective way of communicating with customers via marketing events. For example, some companies are becoming reluctant to take stands at exhibitions because customers can now access so much up-to-date information on the Internet. Brochures printed for the exhibition may not be as current as the organisation's web site!

The sophistication of customer databases also means that individuals can be targeted with personal mailings and communications. Therefore, there is a growing conviction among organisations that expensive and labour-intensive exhibitions may not be the best way of deploying marketing resources. It is better to contact key customers with the right information at appropriate times. However, exhibitions are still popular marketing events for launching new products and promoting others so it is one that most marketers attend at an early stage in their career.

It is important for marketers to appreciate the type of activity that is relevant in their sector. Trade shows are very effective ways of communicating with large numbers of customers in the b2b market whereas service organisations would be more likely to use corporate hospitality to communicate with customers. The not-for-profit sector relies more on direct mailings and business to consumer (b2c) might employ more sales promotions and exhibitions.

Setting SMART objectives

Objectives are also known as goals or targets and represent what needs to be achieved. Having decided to hold a marketing event the first step in the planning process is to decide what objectives are to be set. This makes it easier to evaluate the effectiveness of the event – was it worth the outlay of resources? If you have invested time and effort then you need to decide whether it was well spent.

Measuring the achievement of objectives also provides information for future planning. For example, if the exhibition did not lead to any sales within six months then it may not be worth taking a stand in the future. However, before taking that decision a lot more information needs to be gathered to help the marketer decide whether it was the wrong event or whether the plan was poorly executed – was the stand in the wrong place, staff inadequately briefed etc.?

You may be familiar with the acronym SMART. This stands for:

Specific.
Measurable.
Achievable.
Relevant.
Timed.

Objectives must be specific so everyone knows what they are aiming for. It is not good practice to set a salesperson a general objective simply to increase sales because that individual would immediately want to ask. 'By how much?', 'Which products?', 'How long have I got?' It is possible to measure an increase in sales and it is a relevant goal but an increase of one extra sale would meet this target and that is clearly not significant. A specific objective would be:

'To increase sales revenues of Product A by 2% within six months'.

One further comment from the salesperson might be that it is an impossible target because Product A is in decline and facing fierce and increasing competition from better quality, same price rivals. In other words it is not achievable. In this situation the individual would probably not make much effort because the goal is unrealistic and unlikely to be achieved. Therefore, objectives must be challenging but achievable, otherwise they demotivate rather than inspire!

Planners also use the term 'aims' to describe the overall purpose of events. The two words are often used interchangeably but aims are not as specific as objectives. In the above example the aim set might be to increase total sales by 3.5% over the next twelve months. Specific objectives can then be set for each product so the individual can plan activities to meet these as progress points towards the overall aim.

Activity 5.1: SMART objectives

What aims and objectives might be set for the following events?

How can SMART objectives be set?

Compare your answers with those of fellow students and colleagues.

i)   Press conference held by a government department to announce the results of an enquiry.

ii)   National sales meeting for the organisation's sales force and managers.

The importance of planning

Once SMART objectives have been set the next question to ask yourself is, 'How do I do that?' This is what is meant by planning. A plan is a statement of who will do what, when, where and how to achieve the result required. It is a series of tasks that need to be scheduled so there are some immediate questions that need to be considered:

- What tasks need to be completed?
- Why is this important for me, my manager, the marketing function and the organisation?
- What is the overall timescale?
- What resources are available?
- Where will the work be done?
- How will progress be measured?
- How will information be shared?
- How will communication be managed?
- Has it been done before – what has been learnt from this experience?

For complex events a project team might be appointed but for smaller events, such as a press conference, one person would probably co-ordinate the planning and organisation of the event, drawing on additional resources as required.

Planning requires a structured approach to ensure deadlines are met and relevant people informed of progress so they can organise their own work to fit in with the demands of the plan.

The planning process

Planners use a series of steps to move them from where they are at the start to where they want to be:

Steps in the planning process	Purpose
Setting aims and objectives.	To define overall purpose for all involved and identify required outcomes.
Identifying main tasks.	To ensure that major tasks are planned into the schedule and to assist with identification of resources required to achieve the plan.
Scheduling task completion.	To programme completion so deadlines are met and progress towards the final completion date is maintained.
Defining communication strategy.	To construct a schedule for team meetings to review progress and make decisions about future activities. To identify a reporting structure and organise how information is to be gathered and disseminated to the team and other relevant people such as external agencies.
Auditing resources.	To check what resources are required and availability including people, equipment, materials, finance and information. To set budgets and allocate costs within the budgets set. To define roles and responsibilities for everyone involved.

Steps in the planning process	Purpose
Checking progress.	To set up systems to monitor and control completion of activities. To ensure deadlines are met and shortfalls identified and overcome at the earliest possible time.
Measuring achievement of results.	To identify ways of measuring achievement of aims and objectives. Measurement may take place over a set period of time after the event.
Evaluating results.	To check effectiveness – what was achieved and what was not. To analyse results and identify lessons that can be learnt for the future.

Figure 5.1: Planning steps

When organising marketing events, detailed plans will be set to ensure that each task is achieved at the right time. Decisions need to be made at each step to determine the best course of action. These decisions include those made at the commencement of activities and those made as a result of the monitor and review process.

Evaluating options when decision making

For each decision there may be different options to consider so the right people will need to meet to discuss these and evaluate each before deciding on the best option.

The original aims and objectives provide the guidelines for decision makers. They need to identify which option contributes most towards achievement of the objectives. For example, to gain most press and news coverage for an outlet launch the decision might be taken to hire a celebrity for the opening rather than a local official or company director. Hence costs are allocated for this in the budget plan.

The following table is a useful way of comparing different options by identifying what each involves in terms of cost, people, time and quality. Examples of the relevant questions to ask are shown in the first column.

Option	Cost	People	Time	Quality
Option 1.	What are the direct and indirect costs – how accurately can total expenditure be estimated? Can cost be justified?	Who needs to be involved? Are they available?Are they willing and able?	Is it achievable or feasible in the timescale allowed?	Is this a quality option? Will the organisation's quality reputation be enhanced or diminished?
Option 2.				
Option 3.				

Figure 5.2: Comparing alternative options

The option finally selected should be the one with the most pay-offs and the least penalties. It is rare that there is only one option; usually there are several, each with benefits and disadvantages attached. This is one of the main reasons for using a team approach to planning. Through pooling all knowledge and skills available within the team to weigh up the pros and cons of each option, it is possible to make the best decision.

Scheduling

Once the planner has identified the tasks that must be performed then a schedule for completion can be drawn up. Further information is required on the activities that make up that task, the time that must be allowed for each one, the order in which they need to happen and the degree of overlap that can occur. Some activities can take place simultaneously, while others are dependent on the outcome of an earlier activity.

The easiest way to present a schedule is to use the form of a Gantt chart. This lists activities on a vertical scale and time on a horizontal one as shown below. The example is the production of a press pack for the press conference mentioned in Activity 5.1.

Task: Production of press pack. Start date: Completion date:						
	Week1	Week 2	Week 3	Week 4	Week 5	Week 6
Complete design brief	░					
Brief printers	░					
Brief contributors	░					
Compile copy		░	░			
Proof copy			░			
Organise pictures	░	░				
Proof final design			░	░		
Agree final print proof				░		
Print and deliver					░	
Check finished product						░

Figure 5.3: A Gantt chart

The chart is a simple means of giving everyone an overview of the planned activities and making sure people understand how their contribution fits into the complete picture. When drawing up the schedule it is a good idea to allow for some delays.

Organising resources

The best plan will fail if sufficient resources are not put into it. The 6Ms framework is one that can be used to help audit resources when developing a plan. 6Ms stands for:

Men – people are required to carry out the tasks and activities but also of use is their collective knowledge, skills and experiences.

Money – this may represent a major constraint for planners; it is most unusual to work with an unlimited budget.

Materials – the physical items that are required to make the plan work, such as the information pack for the press conference.

Machines – the equipment required to make the plan work, such as microphones for the press conference.

Minutes – time must be allocated to carry out the planned activities, and estimates of time requirements are needed for scheduling.

Measurements – it is essential to determine how to measure effectiveness when the objectives are set.

Activity 5.2: Decision, decisions

Visit www.venuefinder.com and make a list of the main services provided for event organisers.

Why might this be a useful site if the size of the budget was a major constraint?

Summary of planning

There is a very useful planning framework that can be used with the 6Ms to remind planners of the overall process. This is SOST, which stands for:

Situation – what is the overall purpose of the plan and the context within which this has arisen?

Objectives – what needs to be achieved?

Strategy – how will it be achieved?

Tactics – what needs to happen to make it work?

Imagine that you have been asked to organise a VIP visit to one of your organisation's manufacturing plants which makes biscuits. You might use SOST to help you make notes when preparing to plan for the event.

Situation.	The party is made up of the local Member of Parliament (MP) and three local councillors. Three journalists and a camera crew will also accompany the party. They wish to tour the new production lines on their first day of operation, Monday 5th March. The visit is timed for 1 hour, starting at 10.30am. They would like to talk to the plant manager, operations manager, supervisors and production operatives.
Objectives.	To demonstrate use of the latest production technology to manufacture Scottish shortcakes (can be observed).To gain publicity for the new plan locally and nationally that will enhance the quality reputation of the organisation (can be measured). NB: Make sure objectives are measurable so achievement can be recognised.
Strategy.	Organise a production run to coincide with the visit. Arrange for key personnel to attend, and brief everyone involved. Organise a tour that demonstrates the complete process and the equipment in operation. Make arrangements for filming to take place at strategic areas in the plant.
Tactics.	Liaise with contact in the MP's office to confirm arrangements for arrival, tour and departure. Communicate with journalists and camera crew to confirm arrangements and any special requirements. Confirm visitors' names and status with security. Briefings for all staff to be carried out one week before the event and arrangements confirmed the day before. Confirm production schedule with production manager and tour arrangements. Identify photo opportunities. Organise protective clothing for visit – check all sizes available. Provide photo opportunities with key personnel and of the finished product. Refreshments (tea, coffee and shortcakes) to be served following the tour in the hospitality suite in the new plant. Organise product gift packs and information packs for journalists.

Figure 5.4: Using SOST as a planning tool

The above notes can then be used to draw up a plan for the event. Use the 6Ms framework to organise resourcing of the plan.

You may also be familiar with SOSTAC as a planning tool where A = Action and C = Control.

The planning cycle

Planning is a continuous process. When we go on holiday, even if we visit the same resort each year we make a new plan using our knowledge and experience from previous years to make the next holiday even more enjoyable. We learn from experience and that can be represented by a cycle as in Figure 5.5.

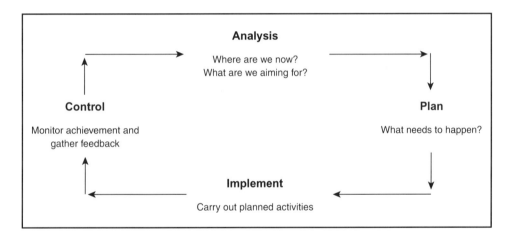

Figure 5.5: The planning cycle

Having analysed the situation and set objectives, a detailed plan is drawn up. During implementation various controls, such as monitoring and progress meetings, are used to ensure it achieves the objectives set. During the lifetime of the plan, feedback is gathered on how well activities and tasks were completed to help the final evaluation of effectiveness. This provides information for the next planner facing a similar situation.

Budgets and budgeting

When organising an event you will probably be working to a budget so you will need to know what your costs will be to make sure that your total expenditure does not go over the sum agreed. There are situations when you may be allowed to spend more than was originally agreed. This might be because there are future benefits to be gained by doing so.

For example, when preparing for an exhibition you may find that the stand is damaged and beyond repair. Purchasing a new one takes you over budget because a cost was not allocated to this when the budget was prepared. However, the decision may be made to put money in for this because it will be useful for the future.

Alternatively, if money cannot be made available for this you might be asked to get estimates for the hire of a suitable stand and money allocated in next year's budget for a new one. Although in the long term it may have been more cost effective to purchase, if the money cannot be diverted from another budget to cover the unexpected expense, then the next best option, such as hiring, has to be taken.

It is also important to note that there will be direct costs – those that can be readily identified and estimated fairly accurately – and indirect costs. In the example of planning an exhibition, the latter might relate to the research carried out to get estimates, time taken to brainstorm ideas for a more creative and innovative approach to last year, and lots of other activities that are not formally planned but which arise as the plan is implemented.

There will also be unexpected costs, as previously mentioned, so if you are drawing up a budget then allow a cushion for this. If you are given the budget then make sure you do not spend it all at once so there is no contingency fund available! For example, if you had estimated that printed materials for the exhibition would cost £5,000 and you managed to get what was required for £4,000, then you could offer £1,000 towards the cost of a new stand, so that the full sum does not have to be taken from elsewhere.

The budget should have been drawn up to allow for reasonable expenditure and based on previous experience. Many organisations attend exhibitions regularly so will have a good idea what the overall cost is likely to be. If you have been set the task of estimating expenditure, the first thing to do is to identify what money needs to be spent on and to make a list of what is the probable cost of each item. It is also useful to note the maximum figure that you feel is justified for each. A typical budget breakdown for exhibiting at an exhibition is shown in Figure 5.6.

Costs	Probable figure	Maximum figure
Booking fee.		
Pre-event publicity.		
Stand.		
Graphics.		
Audio visuals.		
Set-up costs at event.		
Publicity materials, brochures.		
Staff.		
Refreshments.		
Hosting seminar or hospitality event during show.		
Post-event publicity.		
Indirect costs.		
Totals.		

Figure 5.6: Budget breakdown for attending an exhibition

Decisions on how to allocate costs should be linked to what you want to achieve from the event. It is also important that the budget identifies how money will be spent as accurately as possible so get realistic estimates and quotations from reliable and well-respected suppliers. A final reason for estimating expenditure is related to the original decision to attend the exhibition. If costs have risen significantly then it may not be worth attending, and alternative ways of achieving the objectives can be sought.

Activity 5.3: Working with budgets

You have been asked to give a short presentation to a new group of marketing assistants on cost control when managing a project such as the organisation of a marketing event. Prepare a few slides to help you get your main points across.

Checklist for venue appraisal

The next Session considers how to organise and host events that will be memorable and appropriate. An exciting venue, such as a national museum, racecourse, castle or cricket ground is one of the ways that this can be achieved. However, when planning the event it is important to determine whether the venue can accommodate your requirements. The checklist below provides an easy way of checking overall suitability.

Dimension	Checklist
Size.	■ Can all delegates be accommodated comfortably? ■ Does the venue allow delegates to move around without bottlenecks and delays? ■ Are dining and refreshment areas of appropriate size? ■ Are meeting rooms, seminar rooms and conference hall appropriate sizes?
Facilities.	■ Is there sufficient parking within convenient distance? ■ Is there the right range of rooms available for all activities, conveniently located? ■ Does the venue have appropriate security? ■ Are facilities available for those with special needs? ■ Are catering arrangements adequate? ■ What leisure facilities are available? ■ Are they appropriate? ■ Are they of the right standard? ■ Is there air conditioning in every room?

Dimension	Checklist
Equipment.	■ Range and availability? ■ Is there technical support if needed? ■ What is included in the hire of facilities? ■ Can own equipment be transported to meeting rooms etc.?
Accessibility.	■ Is location convenient to ensure minimum travelling time for those attending? ■ Good road, rail and air links? ■ Is there a VIP entrance?
Cost.	■ Are costs within budget? ■ What discounts are offered? ■ Can prices be negotiated?

Figure 5.7: Venue appraisal

You can add to the above list specific questions that you need to ask according to the event you are organising. For example, if arranging the product launch of a new car you will need to check if there is an appropriate setting for photographs and room for photographers. Do not assume that the venue owners will be delighted to have your high performance product driving over their well-manicured lawns!

Some criteria may be more important than others. For example, is it more important that the venue be near a major international airport than that the bedrooms are the largest of the different venues you are appraising?

Activity 5.4: Venue dilemma

Look at the following information on two venues.

If you had been asked to organise a two-day (Tuesday and Wednesday) residential conference for 100 field staff working for a company selling household products, which would you select and why?

The conference begins at 10am on the first day (Registration from 8.30am) and ends at 3pm on the second day. Both venues are within budget. The two days will be very intensive with little time for relaxation for the delegates, some of whom will be travelling long distances to attend. Some (20% of delegates) will require overnight accommodation the night before the conference.

Hotel A	Conference centre B
Used for the meeting in the previous 2 years (fantastic feedback from delegates) and has good working relationship with conference manager.	Never used before but highly recommended from a reliable source.
Size appropriate – conference will take over the whole hotel, beautiful grounds.	Conference can be accommodated easily – large site with assault course in the grounds.
Easy road links but rail is difficult, which some delegates noted as a problem last year.	Easy rail and road links.
Facilities excellent and appropriate, basic equipment with more specialist equipment hired from very reliable external source.	Facilities excellent and appropriate, conference halls and meeting rooms fully equipped with latest technology.
Excellent leisure facilities – gym and pool.	Limited leisure facilities – gym only.

Hotel A	Conference centre B
Discounts offered to loyal customers.	Discounts negotiable.
24hr delegate rate £105 all inclusive.	24 hr delegate rate £107 all inclusive.
Bed & Breakfast rate £75 for weekdays.	Bed & Breakfast rate £55 for weekdays.

Case Study – The great debate

When branch Continuing Professional Development Advisers (CPD Advisers) got together with Chartered Institute of Personnel and Development (CIPD) Membership Development staff for their annual conference focusing on continuing professional development, the event took a novel approach to previous years.

Rather than taking a formal structure with lengthy speeches and PowerPoint presentations, the two-day event, based at a hotel in Kenilworth, Warwickshire, was designed as a more interactive conference where the 70 participants could collaborate in groups to share best practice and develop ideas for supporting members' CPD activities.

A major part of the event was taken up by group-based activities, designed and facilitated by Jean Floodgate and David Lock of Inside Outreach. As a member of the Institute's CPD working party, Floodgate collaborated closely with Christine Williams, CIPD Membership Development Manager, and others to structure the interactive event so that discussion and debate would be based on relevant work experiences and would generate real results.

A cross-section of participants was invited to form an initial design group in order to fix the purpose and overall content of the conference. The process decided upon involved mixed groups of eight people from the branches, the working party and the Institute. They worked as self-managed teams to discuss key issues. This was designed to encourage collaboration and co-operation. Ideas from each team were then fed back to the group as a whole for further debate and to help develop a shared vision for future CPD activities.

There was also a graffiti wall where participants could post questions, thoughts and comments throughout the conference and create a source of discussion.

"This participatory, yet structured approach enabled everyone to contribute their views in developing the CPD agenda," Floodgate said. Participants were encouraged to be creative – particularly in developing their vision of the future – and it meant they could have fun in the process.

"Our aims by the end of the conference was that advisers would have had the chance to establish stronger networks of shared knowledge and understanding," Williams said. "We wanted to identify and understand what is changing, the implications for membership and new ways of supporting the Institute's standards through CPD and branch events."

Feedback from the event indicated that participants welcomed this novel approach. "Working in small groups helped us to discuss and resolve points straightaway. We all took responsibility, which helped us to achieve a lot more than in the past," said one adviser.

As well as achieving greater awareness of continuing professional development, nearly a quarter of the delegates highlighted the importance of networking. There was also a sense of a shared strategy of moving the CPD agenda forward.

Williams stressed that the conference had shown that, by sharing expertise and experience, branch advisers could play a pivotal role in developing practical CPD strategies at local level. A number of people were interested (for their own CPD) in the participative approach, which is based on 'whole systems' thinking and large group engagement methods.

Source: Originally published in *People Management*, 10th January 2002 and reproduced with permission.

Questions

1. The article highlights the collaborative approach taken by the people involved in designing the conference programme and content. How important do you think it is that event organisers also work closely with these people?

2. What difficulties might planners encounter when organising such a 'different' event?

3. What suggestions might you make regarding the venue to support the nature of the event to enhance success?

SUMMARY OF KEY POINTS

- Effective planning starts with setting SMART objectives so everyone knows what needs to be achieved.

- Identify what needs to be achieved and by when to create a schedule of activities for your plan.

- Ensure you can resource your plan – use tools such as 6Ms to check the different category of resources that will be required.

- Spend the budget effectively by estimating what costs you will incur and how to control spending. Ensure the estimates and quotations you obtain are as accurate as possible.

- Consider what might go wrong and add contingency to your plan.

- One way of creating a more creative event is to select an exciting venue; however, it must appropriate to the requirements of the event. Use a venue checklist to help check whether a venue holds all the essential criteria you need. Some criteria may be more important than others, so ensure that you understand the relative weighting of each before making a final selection.

Improving and developing own learning

The following projects are designed to help you to develop your knowledge and skills further by carrying out some research yourself. Feedback is not provided for this type of learning because there are no 'answers' to be found but you may wish to discuss your findings with colleagues and fellow students.

Project A

You may have been involved in setting your own objectives for your personal and professional development when starting out on the Certificate in Marketing. Review these now. Were they SMART? Are you on track to achieve these within the timescale set? Do you need to set fresh objectives?

Did you make a development plan? Review this in line with your new or amended objectives and those you still have to achieve. What barriers to achievement have you encountered and how have these been overcome? Are resources available to help you achieve you plan? If not what can be done about this?

Have you recently attended an exhibition as a representative for your organisation or been involved in the planning of such an event? What objectives were set? Were decisions made about who to target? How successful was the event? How was that measured in the short term and over the longer term? If you have not been involved in exhibitions talk to a fellow student or colleague who has to learn from their experiences.

Project B

Consider a recent project you were involved in which went over budget. How was the budget set? Was all expenditure (direct and indirect costs) accurately forecast? How effectively was expenditure managed? What improvements can you suggest to ensure a realistic budget is set with better monitoring of expenditure next time?

Project C

Visit www.e-bulletin.com and note the information available for event organisers. If you were tasked with finding a venue for an international conference how useful would this site be? Can you check floor plans of venues (search for Alexandra Palace which is a good example of this). What information is available on exhibitions and other events? What other services are available?

Feedback on activities

Activity 5.1: SMART objectives

i)   Press conference held by a government department to announce the results of an enquiry – objectives are timed by the time of the event although achievement needs to be measured at a later date once reports are published in the national press. Note that actions are specific, timed, can be measured(coverage given by media targeted), are relevant and should be achievable as a press conference has been called. If you had set these objectives you would check that resources were available:

- To disseminate news releases to national press (named publications) 2 days before the event and immediately following the event.

- To communicate key messages in news releases (identify key points) to national press.

- To reply to recent speculation (outline issues that need to be addressed) in national press in the news releases.

ii) National sales meeting for the organisation's sales force and managers. Note specific actions are identified with timings, all are relevant, can be measured – for example outcomes from focus groups – and are achievable. Again assuming sufficient resources have been identified:

- To reward an exceptionally successful year – overall results 10% above budgeted figures (identify specific rewards).

- To launch new product to sales force (introduce product ready for sales launch in one month's time).

- To gather feedback from sales force (specific areas for feedback such as review of reporting procedures) using focus group format.

- To enable training required for new product launch to take place.

Activity 5.2: Decision, decisions

This is an international site so marketers can search for venues in their own country and internationally. The main services offered are the ability to search for venue via:

- Location – within specified distances of major towns and cities, airports, motorways etc.

- Delegate rate – useful if money is tight!
- Size.
- Equipment.
- Supplier's list – products and services from badges to security services.
- Links to industry associations.

Activity 5.3: Working with budgets

Setting a budget
- Identify costs.
- Obtain realistic estimates.
- Agree importance of each cost.
- Add a figure for indirect and unexpected costs.
- Note maximum spend for each cost.

Cost control
- Inform team of cost constraints at start.
- Monitor planned/actual expenditure closely.
- Review variances.
- Inform relevant people of potential overspend.
- Revise budget figures to prevent overspend.

Post-event evaluation
- Review actual against estimated spend.
- Identify reasons for over/underspend.
- Justify overspend.
- Evaluate cost effectiveness of event.
- Learn lessons for the future!

Activity 5.4: Venue dilemma

It can be appreciated that as either venue is within budget then the marketer may select Hotel A because it was a hit with those who attended last year's conference. In addition, it may also be possible to negotiate more substantial discounts because it is a repeat booking. This might offset the additional costs that using Hotel A over Hotel B will incur – £400 for the 20 delegates requiring overnight accommodation as the B&B package is more expensive by £20 per person and the conference equipment hire as Hotel A has limited equipment. The other downside of Hotel A is that for delegate travelling by rail their journey will not be as easy as for Hotel B.

However, the Conference manager at Hotel B might be eager to get a new customer and offer substantial discounts and match the lower day delegate offered by Hotel B – thus saving £400. This venue has not been used before so it will need to be checked out more thoroughly than Hotel B.

When selecting an option, cost is important but must be considered in conjunction with other factors. A cheaper venue might not be as comfortable and so lead to delegate dissatisfaction making the event less successful overall. The marketer must be prepared to negotiate with conference managers at venues but be honest. Do not say that you can get an alternative venue at 50% less because you will lose credibility.

Session 6

Organising events

Introduction

Event organising is now a separate industry in its own right but many small organisations still do this mainly in-house, using specialist expertise or services to fill the gaps in their own skills. Since the success of the activity depends partly on the amount of publicity it attracts, it is important that marketers learn to be creative and innovative.

This might mean an unusual venue as discussed in the previous Session but could also apply to the individual activities that make up the event or a surprise guest! There are no limits on the imagination as you have probably noticed from reading reports in the marketing press! The previous Session concentrated on planning one explores implementation of plans, evaluation and hosting.

Many organisations operate in a global market so marketers need to understand how to host events for international visitors. Finally we will consider again why it is important to evaluate the success of all marketing activities and how to learn from this exercise.

LEARNING OUTCOMES

At the end of this Session you will be able to:

- Describe the scope of individuals' roles in marketing: meetings, conferences, exhibitions, outdoor shows, outlet launches and press conferences.

- Identify alternative and innovative approaches to a variety of marketing arenas and explain criteria for meeting business objectives.

- Explain how an organisation should host visitors from other cultures and organising across national boundaries.

Organising exhibitions

The previous Session reviewed the planning phase so now it is time to look at the detail of putting plans into practice. The example of organising an exhibition is used to illustrate the level of detail required.

- **Understanding event objectives**

  Having made the decision to take a stand at the exhibition you should be aware of why you want to be there. Therefore, before starting to organise the event check your understanding of the objectives because the decisions you make about allocating costs should be linked to what you need to achieve from the investment. The objectives might include reminding customers of what you can do for them, targeting a specific group, increasing subscriptions, generating sales leads, making new contacts, and checking out the competition. You will also need to make sure that you can measure achievement of these to inform post-event evaluation.

- **Publicity**

  Spectacular displays and expensive hospitality events are wasted if people do not come to see you. Mailshot potential clients and loyal customers – using email if appropriate – to let them know where you are. An incentive to visit is usually a good way of increasing visitor numbers – a free draw is rather old hat so try and think of something more creative. You will probably be provided with some free tickets so send these to key accounts to save them pre-registering.

  When booking the stand enquire about opportunities for sponsorship to ensure your name is more prominently displayed than your competitors in the exhibition guide and elsewhere. Reserve your stand position early to ensure maximum choice. If you regularly exhibit at the same show then confirm your site at the previous event!

  Check with the exhibition press officer the date of the exhibition preview. When you know which press and broadcast media are previewing, provide the editors with all relevant information. You may wish to invite specific journalists to visit your stand. Go through the press office if they are making these arrangements and provide an informative but concise press pack.

  Keep in touch with the exhibition press officer throughout the show to obtain information about arrangements for official opening, special events and exhibition newsletters. If a visiting VIP party has an interest in your products and services, propose that your stand is included in the official tour. During the exhibition there will be daily publicity briefings and bulletins so exhibitors are informed about special events and given details of high profile visitors.

  Prepare exhibition follow-up letters before the event so they can be sent promptly once they have been personalised. Also follow up all press leads and use the event to extend your personal network of contacts. Contact the editors of any journals that featured your stand or products to discuss possible follow-up articles or interviews. Evaluate the media interest in your company and use this information to further your media relations.

■ Stand design and set-up

Few organisations will design a stand for one event due to the cost but if you do need to organise this start well in advance of the event – at least 6 months beforehand. Provide the designers with branded literature and information on organisation vision and values. A cheaper alternative to custom-built stands is a modular stand and there are many creative and innovative designs to choose from. Even if your organisation does have a stand in storage it will need to be checked for damage or may need modification if there have been changes in brand image since it was used last.

Make appropriate use of new technology to 'impress' visitors and show off new products to best advantage. The digital age allows organisations to mount exhibitions that allow the visitor to enjoy a more interactive experience through the use of touch screen technology and Internet enabled computer terminals. Videos are another useful means of displaying your products and demonstrations may be appropriate. Printed brochures will also be required but final information about a new product has to be available some time in advance for these, whereas electronic data can be changed or input easily at short notice. Ensure adequate supply of electricity and telephone lines to 'plug in and log on' will have to be carefully worked out. Many disasters occur because there are inadequate sockets etc.

One of the most straightforward and least expensive ways of producing graphics for your stand is to use PowerPoint. The software, produced by Microsoft, enables the presenter to create a slide show on a computer that can then be projected onto a large screen if required. It is very easy to use and the latest versions allow very sophisticated presentations to be produced in a relatively short time. Company logos, graphs, charts and pictures can be incorporated into the presentation so it is exceptionally versatile. The original version can be easily adapted to meet the needs of specific audiences so it is a very versatile solution.

Ensure that you know the exact measurements for dimensions of your stand when booking space at the exhibition. This tends to be square or rectangular but your exhibition stand may be octagonal. In addition consider all the fixtures, fittings, equipment and staff that need room to move – let alone the visitors. They will not want to stand too close to videos but will want close-up views of demonstrations. Finally remember to add some storage space for brochures and personal effects of stand staff. An untidy stand is a real turn-off for most visitors as is lots of empty space!

■ **People**

Everyone representing the company should be well briefed about the aims and objectives, products and the organisation. You cannot send your entire sales force and will need some meeters and greeters so make sure that they know how to approach visitors. Inform staff of the dress code – do not rely on their common sense. Remind stand staff to wear comfortable shoes!

Ensure records are kept of visitors and their exact requirements so these can be followed up if not dealt with on the day. Making new contacts is a major reason for many organisations to take a stand at a trade show. Many organisations run competitions or ask visitors to put their business cards into a 'hat' for the chance of winning a prize to gain more contact names – but most of these are unlikely to be useful leads.

Plan a schedule for the duration of the exhibition to cover main marketing activities, roles and responsibilities for personnel hosting the exhibition stand. People need to be able to take frequent breaks. On no account allow eating and drinking on the stand unless you are providing hospitality for visitors.

■ **On the day**

Check the day before that the stand has been erected correctly and that all printed materials and giveaways have arrived. This will ensure that you can take your time arranging the exhibition and making sure all boxes and rubbish are cleared away. Most exhibitions last several days so make sure that someone takes this responsibility each morning if you are not there yourself. Emphasise to staff the importance of keeping displays clean and tidy. Often it is the way that products are set out that sells them, rather than expensive literature. Visitors will leave with bag loads of literature and rarely get round to reading it all. Eye-catching displays attract attention, which is the first step to getting visitors onto your stand. Then it is up to you! Ensure staff are well trained in dealing effectively with browsers and customers.

Finally, ensure that information is collected which allows accurate evaluation of the event. It is essential that marketers understand how to learn from experience. Reflecting on what went well, what went wrong and how to make improvements is a key part of the evaluation process. This is discussed in detail towards the end of this Session.

Mobile exhibitions

Mobile exhibitions and roadshows are popular ways of taking a message to people who would not otherwise come to you! Organisations use the latter to communicate messages or disseminate information and training on a personal basis rather than using written communication such as letter or bulletin. Roadshows may take place at a hotel or similar venue or even via a mobile unit.

There are many companies that provide mobile units for displays and exhibitions at outdoor events. Alternatively they can be used to take products and demonstrations to customer premises. Units may contain a number of facilities including office space in addition to exhibition area, video, computer, modem for Internet access and kitchen with fridge.

Activity 6.1: Events checklist

As a marketing executive you have been asked to give a talk to a group of marketing students about organising events. Write a checklist for event organisation that you could provide as a handout. You may wish to break the checklist down into pre- and post- event tasks and on the day tasks.

Activity 6.2: Online exhibitions are a virtual reality

Read the following extract from *Marketing Business*, July/August 2000 and then answer the set questions.

...So although there is no reason to assume that virtual shows will ever replace the real thing, there is a huge debate about the extent to which the Internet can be used to enhance more traditional methods of reaching target audiences.

An interesting example of the joint promotional opportunities within the exhibitions industry is the Training Solutions and IT Training Show. This is the show's fifth year but for the first time it will run as an interactive virtual exhibition as well as the usual terrestrial show at the National Exhibition Centre (NEC) in Birmingham. The show has been created by the NEC show organisers, Brintex, working together with Expocentric.co. According to the organiser of both shows, Frazer Chesterman, this is the first time a commercial trade exhibition will take place online.

The virtual show, which runs from 14th June until 28th July, has been created around the usual NEC event, which runs from 4th-6th July. The opportunity to exhibit at the virtual show will only be open to those exhibiting at the main event. The online show has been designed to enable potential visitors to communicate with company representatives, evaluate products, request information and book face to face appointments for the NEC show. Those who pre-register to visit the NEC show are automatically given free access to the virtual exhibition.

Questions:

1. What are the potential advantages for organisations of virtual exhibiting?

2. What potential disadvantages might there be for virtual exhibitors?

Organising conferences, meetings and outdoor events

The principles discussed above also apply to the organising of these events but some of the different features are discussed below.

■ **Meetings**

Most hotels and conference centres offer meeting rooms for hire that can accommodate small to large meetings. Other common venues include motorway service stations and public houses.

In-house meetings may be half or full day events and are usually held off-site if the organisation wishes to concentrate on the topic and avoid being distracted by events in the workplace. Therefore, the venue must be convenient for all travelling to the meeting, comfortable with facilities such as flip chart, whiteboard (electronic versions are popular), overhead projector, telephone, fax and photocopying support.

External meetings may be large events but the above points still apply. However, in addition you may need to mail out joining instructions for attendees. For in-house meetings email may be the most convenient channel of communication.

- **Conferences**

Conferences again may be in-house events, such as a national sales conference or large, complex events with delegates coming from different organisations and possibly countries. Hosting international events is explored later in the Session.

A conference usually involves a series of talks, lectures or seminars which all delegates may attend with additional activities such as workshops for which delegates split into smaller groups. Often a gala dinner or similar event may be planned to take place one evening. Delegates may also be able to bring partners so a separate programme of leisure activities may need to be arranged for them.

Conference speakers may also have special requirements that need to be accommodated. They will need full information about how their presentation fits into the conference programme and details on how to reach the venue. If not using their own transport they may need to be collected from the airport or railway station. Speakers may also require specialist equipment to deliver their presentation.

For the marketer organising a conference the following information is essential:

- Conference programme.
- Number of delegates attending.
- Speakers and requirements – AV equipment etc.
- Catering requirements.
- Venue requirements.
- Printed material needed – invitations, conference packs etc.

- **Outdoor events**

The range of outdoor events is enormous from outdoor shows such as flower shows and agricultural shows to corporate entertainments such as golf competitions. Each needs to be carefully planned with the weather being a prime consideration. Often large tents, marquees and similar temporary structures are used to house main displays. There may also be additional Health and Safety issues to be taken into account on temporary sites or if sporting activities or similar are involved.

There are many companies that will turn a greenfield site into a bustling show ground with full facilities for the general public and exhibitors. If it is public event on a temporary site, additional security will be required and you will need to notify the relevant authorities about the temporary increase in road and foot traffic.

An Eidophor screen, which is a giant version of CCTV, is often used for large public events such as outdoor concerts and sports events. This extra-large screen is also used for overflow crowds where an event is so popular that the venue is too small to cater for everyone. The action can be relayed to the large screen so everyone has a good view of the main action, no matter how far away they are.

Outlet launches

A major event for organisations and one that will, hopefully, attract a lot of media attention. Like many of the events mentioned above, planning will begin many months before the day of the launch.

Celebrities are often invited to open outlets officially, and may be a local celebrity or a household name depending on the occasion. To get national media coverage a national celebrity would be chosen, whereas for a very local opening, such as a new wing to a hospital a famous previous patient might be asked to 'cut the tape'. It is important that the figure chosen has popular appeal and is not a controversial figure, otherwise the media coverage may concentrate on this rather than the real story.

In addition to arrangements for the event, special consideration must be given to photo opportunities for the media and access to key personnel and celebrities to maximise potential coverage.

Timing is very important for this type of activity because it is usually a brief event compared to others. The media will be present for as short a time as possible so everything must be ready for them. Arrangements must also be made for the general public who will want to come along to see the celebrity and other Very

Important Persons (VIPs). Therefore, on the day, the organiser will need to ensure the programme is carefully co-ordinated and proceeds according to plan and on time.

News releases will be given immediately prior to the event and following the opening, so that information is available to the media who do not wish to attend the opening but who may wish to feature it if there is sufficient interest in the outlet or the celebrity. Don't forget that it is equally important to communicate this event – and others – internally to the people of the organisation.

Event evaluation

It is important to know how successful an event has been in terms of achieving its aims and objectives and whether it was money well spent. Some events are easier to assess than others because there is a quantitative means of measurement. For example, you can count the number of visitors to an exhibition stand, new contacts made, sales leads and orders taken. However, this does not provide the full picture. New contacts may never place an order and may have taken up valuable time, so existing customers were not given sufficient time when they visited the stand and found rival companies more welcoming!

As previously mentioned when setting objectives, the means of measurement will be set up and may be taken over a set time so, for example, the number of leads converted to sales can be quantified. Only then can a full and accurate evaluation of the event be made and the information be recorded for the use of future event planners.

Qualitative evaluation from key staff taking part is also very useful. Exhibition staff will be able to give feedback on how easy it was to deal with the flow of people visiting the stand, what people were most interested in – product demonstration, video etc. – and other relevant factors so improvements can be made for the future.

Many corporate events are very difficult to evaluate. Corporate hospitality may be provided, with the main purpose being to build customer relationships by getting to know people better in a more informal setting and to reward loyalty. However, these are long-term objectives and one event will contribute but may not produce an identifiable result. In this case the experience and judgement of the marketing manager is a key factor in the evaluation, but it may be that annual events take place because they have always happened and no one has challenged whether the money could be better spent elsewhere!

Activity 6.3: Money well spent?

Read the following extract taken from *Marketing Business*, April 2000 and write some notes to help you prepare a presentation to marketing students on the importance of evaluating events. How might you use the figures quoted to illustrate your main points?

Corporate hospitality still enjoys a big chunk of the marketing budget – some £3,330m is spent on event marketing annually – but whether or not this money is spent wisely or not is another story. According to research commissioned by event marketing company, McMenemy Hill, an alarming portion is still being wasted through lack of strategic planning. The survey spoke to marketing decision makers in 77 UK companies and found that only 34% evaluated marketing events against their objectives, while 35% indicated that there was no evaluation at all. Only half the companies surveyed had a centralised annual plan for events and an alarming 72% cited the personal preference of management as an important determinant when choosing an event.

"Perhaps because events tend to be seen as part of other marcomms tools, such as advertising or PR, they are not really used to their true potential," says Chris Hill, joint Managing Director of McMenemy Hill. "There is a poor understanding of what events can achieve."

Press conferences

Organisations use press releases to communicate information and these are sent to editors and made available to other interested parties. They may give a press briefing when a statement is read out by a key figure when it is important to be seen to comment on situations, but don't want to answer questions.

Press conferences (sometimes referred to as receptions) are organised to communicate directly with journalists and to answer questions. The organisation will take the time to do this because it is easier to ensure the consistency of the message. Information given via press releases and briefings is more open to interpretation because there is no question and answer session where understanding could be assessed and ambiguous points clarified. Increasingly, large gatherings are also filmed by the broadcast media. These events represent significant opportunities for the organisations to communicate and may be called for a number of reasons, including:

- To respond to a crisis.
- To disseminate information regarding significant business achievement or progress.
- To introduce new key personnel.
- To give information about forthcoming events.
- To explain why a controversial decision has been taken.
- To put bad news into context – so-called 'damage limitation'.

They may be hastily convened if there is a crisis situation such as an unexpected disaster, or planned in advance if announcing news about people. As with all the events mentioned so far they must be carefully planned and evaluated. The event will be of short duration and those taking part will need to be carefully briefed about what they can say and how to answer questions. The press will want as much information as possible that is relevant to the event so press packs are essential. They will want to take photographs so the venue must provide for this. In addition it must be easily accessible because unless it is a newsworthy disaster, journalists may find other, more interesting events to attend.

Activity 6.4: Managing press conferences

Working with a group of fellow students or colleagues, draw up a bullet point list of good practice when organising press conferences.

If you can, check your ideas with a marketing executive who regularly organises and attends press conferences.

Hosting international events

When hosting international events the marketer needs to cater for the demands of different cultures and recognise that delegates and visitors will be travelling from long distances. A simple checklist, such as the one below, can be used to ensure no important details are overlooked:

Dimension	Check
Venue.	Are there good rail, road and air links? Is the venue experienced in catering for international visitors?

Dimension	Check
Date & time.	Is the date appropriate for all cultures – public holidays, religious festivals? How long should event registration be open to allow people to arrive at convenient times? How can the programme be structured to ensure people can recover from long journeys?
Language.	Are language interpreters are required? What written materials need to be translated and printed for the event?
Cuisine.	Have menus been prepared to cover multicultural needs? What constraints are there to consider when preparing menus for the event?
Dress.	What dress code is appropriate – delegates should be provided with information on whether business dress is required or if they can dress more casually?
Address/Salutation.	Have staff received training on appropriate forms of address?

Figure 6.1: Checklist for hosting international events

Organising events overseas

Use the same planning tools but remember:

- You will be operating in a different time zone so take this into account if needing to speak to local contacts.

- Many hotel chains are international but if using an 'untried' venue seek recommendations or references from your existing network of contacts who may have experience of that particular country.

- Check date and time to ensure that these do not clash with a national festival or holiday.

Use the checklist above to help you identify relevant cultural issues.

Case Study – New dimensions

Live event organisers are playing an increasingly important role in transforming brands from pretty logos, familiar colours and ambitious mission statements, into tangible products and experiences that engage the public on an emotional and practical level.

Examples of consumer brands abound. Wall's ice cream has created a travelling truck for visitors to experience the different colours and tastes of the brand's ice cream range. Cadbury's World now has a travelling exhibition stand to show the brand's history. Trevor Foley, Director General of the Association of Exhibition Organisers (AEO), observes "There is a trend for exhibitors to have bigger and bigger stands to allow visitors to interact with their products and services."

Phil Watton, head of events at Line Up Communications, notes, "Companies are becoming more interested in communicating the essence of the brand through live events. A brand is made up of products, people and physical image. Much of the brand communications that we do is about the emotive element as much as the physicality of the product. The live event scores by combining all those elements and communicating them in a powerful way."

Live events company RPM Communications helped bring the maligned but revamped Marks & Spencer brand to life in a series of British agricultural shows this summer. The shows are a forum for M&S to demonstrate its support of British agriculture and to emphasise its family appeal. RPM has created a 'brand experience' consisting of a double-deck store-like environment to showcase the best in M&S food, home and clothing ranges.

As visitors enter the mobile 'store' they are met with an ambient sound of satisfied shoppers talking to each other. On the ground floor, a 50-seat cooking theatre runs demonstrations by renowned chefs. A 'Strawberry Taste Tunnel' provides a strawberry wallpapered walk-through area, playing airy summer music and culminating in a strawberry tasting session. Similar 'experiences' convey brand messages about, for example, the quality of fresh produce and the safety of children's products.

Theatre-based shows are not just limited to consumer markets. According to Watton, exhibitors at business to business shows seeking to make a lasting impression cannot get away with static displays. "With the Internet and people's understanding of interactivity, I think expectations are higher," says Watton, "When visitors see a huge amount of presentation technology, they want to get involved."

Watton believes that this desire to 'try things out' creates an opportunity for brand communicators as people don't tend to retain information when they are only being talked to. Interacting with a product or service makes it that much more memorable, particularly for product launches.

Line Up recently created a brand experience show for Hotpoint, to launch a range of washing machines to trade buyers. At the 'Revolution' experience, staged at The Chain Store show in London's Docklands during May 2000, visitors were guided through several themed and interactive demonstration areas where oversized models, computer animations, video clips, ambient sounds and lighting effects created a sense of being inside the machines. The tour ended in an Internet café looking onto the Millennium Dome to emphasise Hotpoint's positioning as a forward-thinking 21st Century company.

Source: Extract from an article that appeared in *Marketing Business*, July/August 2000.

Questions

1. Why are live events a good way to communicate brand image?

2. If creating such an event, how important do you think it is to work closely with the brand manager and his/her team?

3. What might be the downside for Hotpoint of concluding the tour in a café overlooking the Millennium Dome?

SUMMARY OF KEY POINTS

- If events are to attract maximum publicity they need to be creative and innovative.

- When organising events it is important to brief staff who will be acting as hosts on what needs to be achieved so they can contribute effectively.

- Outdoor events may need contingency built in to cater for alternative arrangements in case the weather leads to cancellation.

- It is important to evaluate events to determine how well objectives were met and provide information for future organisers.

- Managing press relationships is important and properly organised press conferences can enhance the organisation's ability to communicate via the media.

- International events must cater for the needs of a multi-cultural audience and the venue needs to be conveniently located for long distance travellers.

- When organising events overseas you would use the same planning tools but take into account the different time zone and use local contacts for the tasks that need to be done face to face.

Improving and developing own learning

The following projects are designed to help you to develop your knowledge and skills further by carrying out some research yourself. Feedback is not provided for this type of learning because there are no 'answers' to be found but you may wish to discuss your findings with colleagues and fellow students.

Project A

With a group of friends and colleagues discuss the exhibitions that you have attended. Which stands attracted your attention?

Why was this?

Which stands were poorly presented?

What suggestions for improvements can you make?

What 'gimmicks' were used to draw visitors' attention to products?

How many organisations made appropriate use of new technology?

Visit the www.e-bulletin.com web site which provides a guide to exhibitions and events. How useful would this web site be to a marketer working in event management?

Project B

Pre- and post-event publicity is a critical success factor for many organisations. How would you, as a marketer, handle the publicity for the following:

i) Launch of a new car at a national motor trade show.

ii) Opening of a new retail outlet for a national chain of health food stores.

iii) Live exhibition for a snack food manufacturer at an agricultural show.

Review the venues in your area – be creative. Consider stately homes, theme parks sports stadia etc., not just hotels and conference centres, and list which would be suitable for a three day international meeting of 100 delegates including some government officials and ministers.

What are the reasons why you have excluded some of the venues?

Project C

With a group of friends and colleagues discuss the press conferences you have attended or seen televised.

How well organised did they appear to be?

How newsworthy were the events?

How much media coverage did they achieve?

Can you suggest any improvements that might have made them more effective?

Feedback on activities

Activity 6.1: Events checklist

The specific activities that need to be organised will vary according to the nature of the event. The following is a useful reminder but you may wish to write your own for each event.

Pre-event organisation

- Brief project team on aims and objectives, budget, allocate roles and responsibilities.

- Publicity – contact media and arrange news releases.

- Promotion – check advertising and other promotional activities are scheduled etc.

- Arrange for invitations to be sent and responses collated.

- Select venue, check facilities and liaise with event staff.

- Check catering arrangements.

- Make arrangements for necessary equipment to be available.

- Check event materials are ordered.

- Select, brief and train event staff.

- Review event plan and monitor progress at regular intervals.

On the day

- Arrive early to check all arrangements are in place.
- Organise meeters and greeters.
- Give final briefing to event staff.
- Check VIPs, special guests and speakers etc. arrive on time.
- Monitor programme schedule and ensure activities happen on time.
- Thank event staff at the close.
- Check arrangements for 'clearing up' after the event.
- Thank venue staff.
- Check VIPs, special guests and speakers etc. leave on time.
- Collect feedback from appropriate people.
- Collect data and information for evaluation purposes.

Post-event activities

- Follow up media interest.

- Send out follow-up letters, information etc. to visitors.

- Evaluate estimated costs against actual costs and identify reasons for variances.

- Evaluate achievement of objectives and share lessons learnt with appropriate people.

Activity 6.2: Online exhibitions are a virtual reality

1. The potential advantages for exhibiting organisations include:

   - Opportunity to reach more people – broaden their marketplace.

   - Longer duration of exposure – the virtual exhibition is open from 14th June to 28th July.

   - Reaching people at a time that is convenient for them.

   - Does not require expensive manpower.

2. What might potential disadvantages be?

   - Lack of face to face contact with visitors – no opportunity for personal selling.

   - Limited ability to give product demonstrations.

Activity 6.3: Money well spent?

The important points to make are:

- The need to evaluate events.

- Potential to spend budget allocation more effectively.

- The importance of setting measurable objectives.

- The importance of better planning – survey reveals this as a weakness (72% taking part in the survey cited management preference as a means of selecting events!).

- The difficulties of measurement, which may account for the lack of event evaluation.

- The need for continual review of how the event marketing budget is set.

- The opportunities for organisations which can evaluate effectively – around two thirds of companies surveyed, probably many of them your competitors, do not do this or perhaps do it badly.

Use the figures in the article to support your points but put them in perspective. Avoid simply quoting numbers and always identify source and to what the numbers refer.

Activity 6.4: Managing press conferences

Good practice includes:

- Time is short and space may be limited so only invite relevant people.

- Sign guests in so information can be sent to those who didn't attend.

- Choose a convenient time and place for the press, bearing in mind their likely editorial deadlines.

- Keep the party from the host organisation to a minimum to avoid conflicting messages being given and journalists being outnumbered.

- Brief speakers well and schedule a rehearsal if appropriate or possible.

- If the event is pre-planned telephone guests the day before to remind them to attend.

- Make sure everything is ready on the day and goes ahead according to time – journalists cannot afford to be kept waiting!

- If providing refreshments let everyone know in advance what is available and when.

- Have printed information ready for guests to take away and place on company web site.

- Organise photo opportunities.

- If pre-planned, check what else is happening to avoid clashing with other significant or rival events – this simply causes irritation.

Session 7

Working with the media

Introduction

This Session will help marketers understand how to select appropriate media for advertising, PR and promotion. Press and broadcast media and the Internet offer many opportunities to get the message across but it is important that it reaches the right audiences. Scheduling media for advertising will also be explored. Matching media to PR purposes will be explored in Session 8 which covers the promotional mix.

Many marketers also get involved in the design and production of printed materials. Choosing and briefing a designer and printer is essential if this is going to be produced externally but we will also look at how this can be done in-house if required.

LEARNING OUTCOMES

At the end of this Session you will be able to:

- Select media to be used based on appropriate criteria for assessing media opportunities and recommend a media schedule.

- Explain the process for designing, developing and producing printed matter, including leaflets, brochures and catalogues.

Media selection

When selecting a medium to communicate a message there are fundamental considerations such as:

- Environment – is it appropriate?

- Coverage and frequency – can the message be communicated to the target audience at the right time?

- Cost – is it money well spent?

Different media offer different benefits and disadvantages depending on what needs to be achieved. So before a decision can be made, the marketer needs to be aware of the purpose and objectives of the communication. Therefore, before considering criteria for selection it is a good idea to examine the characteristics of the main media categories.

Television

Increasingly popular and cost effective as an increasing number of specialist channels become available enabling marketers to target more specifically. Cable and satellite TV added significantly to the number of channels available but the launch of digital broadcasting has added many more opportunities. Digital broadcasting involves the compression of information so more can be sent in the same bandwidth. In addition the quality of sound and picture are enhanced.

Television offers an ideal channel for communication despite the relatively high costs involved. Viewing figures and audience profiles are available from television companies and independent research organisations such as – British Audience Research Bureau (BARB) – so the schedule can be matched to the product's target audience.

Television offers the opportunity to produce dynamic messages in full colour using many special techniques – at a cost. Interactive TV means that consumers can respond immediately and at their convenience so this is good choice for commercial enterprises. Most broadcasting companies produce very high standard news reports and current affairs programmes creating good opportunities for PR.

The disadvantage is the cost if purchasing prime time slots for advertising. Also many viewers use videos to record programmes that they watch at a later date. They may fast forward the advertisements or use the time to do something else rather than concentrate on commercials. New technical advances mean that commercial breaks need not be recorded, so the viewer never receives the message.

Cinema

Similar to television, it is a creative medium offering good scope for high impact communications. The audience is more likely to see the message but costs can be high. However, accurate targeting is easier because of the audience profiles that go to watch specific genres of film.

Radio

Over the past few years the number of commercial stations catering for specific audiences has made this a more cost-effective channel of communication than it used to be. Radio is a limited medium because picture and movement are not possible but costs are far lower than for other broadcast media.

Many programme editors will provide interview time for speakers who are knowledgeable about topical issues or following the launch of a popular book or film. Many consumers listen to local radio stations when travelling in their car so it is an ideal choice for local advertisers and PR.

Newspaper

Similar to broadcast media messages. Can be targeted at national or local audiences and more specifically by type of reader. Circulation figures and readership surveys are available so effectiveness for broadsheet and popular press can be evaluated.

The cost of advertising depends on publication used and size but can very high in national publications. Advertisements are usually classified according to type so that consumers know where to look. There is limited opportunity to use colour, unless buying space in a colour supplement, making it more difficult to create immediate impact.

Publicity executives measure the success of campaigns by the number of significant mentions or column inches of print. If accurately targeted, press releases can be a very cost-effective way of using print media, especially if the content attracts editorial comment. However, a major disadvantage of this medium is that the organisation does not have direct control over the final message printed because the content will have been interpreted by the journalist writing the copy and made as newsworthy as possible. Therefore, some main points may have lost significance.

Newspaper web sites can prolong exposure as most articles are reproduced in the same format as the printed version. Searchable archives enhance this further but it is worth remembering that this means that bad news as well as good news gets greater exposure.

Magazines and journals

Advertisers can find it very cost effective to use special interest magazines or popular lifestyle magazines that are read by the target audience. There is much more opportunity to use colour and it is usually less expensive than national newspapers.

Advertisers can combine the use of broadcast and print media very effectively by using a strong television advertisement to open the campaign and follow it up by reminders in print. A common way of launching a new product (after the initial burst campaign for the launch of the product), a cost-effective drip campaign can be implemented in appropriate consumer magazines. This is discussed later in the Session.

There are many different categories of magazine from trade journals and professional titles that are subscription-only, to consumer products on almost any subject one can think of!

Many industry specific titles are useful targets for communications as feature articles are a good way of gaining media coverage. Again the organisation may not achieve much control over what appears in the final printed article.

Posters

This medium can have high impact but is mainly static. It offers a broad opportunity rather than a specific targeted one. Advertisers often use posters to reinforce a message that has also appeared elsewhere in the press or on television. Location options for posters are numerous. Product advertisements can be sited close to the relevant retail outlets – near to the point of purchase – making it an ideal medium for supermarkets and manufacturers of consumer goods.

As a relatively inexpensive way of reaching a large number of people this can be a very cost-effective way of communicating short messages. It is popular with governments and public institutions when a broad approach is required.

Activity 7.1: Media merits

Using the information provided so far, and your existing knowledge, compile a table to compare the relative merits of print and broadcast media for marketing promotions.

Internet

The Internet offers enormous potential but is not an easy medium to use. Many people use the Internet to gather information but are nervous about making online purchases for security reasons or because they prefer to examine the product before buying.

Organisation web sites already exist so production time and costs will be less than for television. Banner advertisements can be used to grab attention with a link to other pages detailing product features and benefits. The use of graphics is more limited than television because of the time taken to download.

The Internet offers organisations global opportunities but once visitors have registered, targeted emails can be sent to them. A main benefit of this medium is that information can be updated as often as required whereas print and broadcast campaign messages have to be prepared in advance and cannot be changed at a later date.

A visit to some organisations' web sites will reveal the scope to communicate offered by this new medium. The disadvantage of lack of personal contact is being minimised by technological advances and the development of electronic communication so consumers are sent messages that are tailored specifically to their needs.

Copyright and the Internet

The Copyright Designs and Patents Act 1988 applies to the Internet but it is difficult to apply because it is not classified as a broadcast medium. However, material on the Internet is protected by national and international copyright law, so copyright must be declared if any image or text is copied. For example, online newspapers attach a statement such as '© XXXX 2002. All rights reserved' to all articles reproduced on their web site.

As in existing law the responsibility for copyright infringement lies with the end user. Therefore it is worth noting that even if the copyright permission has been obtained for a print version, it has to be applied for and paid for separately if it is to appear electronically.

Defamation and the Internet

The Internet is considered to be a publication medium in the same way as a book or newspaper. Therefore, defamatory remarks made on the Internet can attract an action for libel if grounds exist. In addition, the global nature of this medium means that a plaintiff may sue in whichever country of the world he or she feels most confident of success.

Activity 7.2: Web alert!

Visit www.cim.co.uk. What use is made of this medium for promoting the Institute and its services to an individual contemplating a career in marketing?

Selection criteria for promotional messages

Having reviewed the characteristics of the different media, the marketer is ready to finalise the choice of medium or media as many campaigns use a multimedia approach. Decision making is based on considering a number of criteria including:

- National, local or regional coverage required.
- Ability to reach target audience.
- Suitability – is it the right place for the product to be 'seen'?
- Frequency and timing – is this appropriate? For example a monthly publication would not be suitable if the campaign required a weekly communication.
- Cost.

Burst and drip advertising campaigns

Burst and *drip* are the terms used to describe the relative impact of advertising campaigns. *Burst* is high impact communication, used at the start of a campaign, whereas *drip* is a lower impact but more frequent communication, used as a follow-through activity.

The argument for using a strong start is the 'concentrate and dominate' one. Therefore, a high impact, creative medium would be used with the consequent impact on the budget. However, customers are fickle, so need reminding, and new product launches need reinforcing, which demands continuity at a lower level.

Media scheduling

The media schedule is the plan covering the use of the media to support a promotions campaign. It identifies the media used, timing and frequency, so resembles a Gantt chart. For example, the media schedule to cover an advertising campaign to support the launch of a new product such as a car would start a few weeks before the launch and continue for a number of weeks after.

	Week 1	Week 2	Week 3	Launch	Week 5	Week 6	Week 7	Week 8	Week 9
Drip campaign									
National newspapers (1/2 and 1/4 pages)									
National TV (primetime, 1 minute slots)									
Burst campaign									
National TV (primetime, 2 minute slots)									
National newspaper colour supplements (full page)									
Appropriate journals (full page, full colour)									

Table 7.1: Burst and drip advertising technique

From the above it can be seen that this is a multimedia campaign. Another way of using different media is to use a layered campaign as shown below.

	Week 1	Week 2	Week 3	Launch	Week 5	Week 6	Week 7	Week 8	Week 9
Multi layered campaign									
National newspapers (1/2 and 1/4 pages)									
National TV (primetime, 1 minute slots)									
Appropriate journals (full page, full colour)									

Table 7.2: Layered advertising technique

Different media are used in turn so appear in the schedule as layers.

Activity 7.3: Fit to burst!

You are working with a team to prepare for the launch of a new perfume in early December. The company sells its products globally and is keen to make a big impression with the new 'his and hers' product, Duo, which will be available for women in a small spray perfume and for men as an aftershave. A full range of body care products will also be launched. Write some brief notes for yourself to take to a meeting that has been called to discuss the media campaign. The product is classed as a 'designer' product and is sold at large stores as a high priced luxury item. It is aimed at young people in the 20-35 year age range with a high disposable income and the company are keen to consider the use of the Internet. Consider budget implications.

Printed materials

These include leaflets, brochures, flyers and catalogues. Organisations may create these in-house using desktop publishing techniques if small quantities are required but more often these are printed externally, even if they are designed in-house.

In order to provide an estimate a printer will require the following information:

- Quantity – once set-up costs are covered, additional quantities can be printed for relatively inexpensive sums so discuss this with the printer. You might also be able to negotiate a discount for certain quantities ordered over a set period of time.
- Paper – what weight and surface finish is required, usually glossy or matt.
- Size – non-standard sizes might increase costs significantly.
- Finishing – whether additional processes such as folding or gluing are required.
- Colour – full colour, two colour, single colour etc.
- Special printing effects – laminating etc.
- Layout including pictures and photographs.
- Date order needs to be delivered – allow plenty of time if using an external designer.

The designer will need a creative brief which must detail purpose, company image and the message that the organisation wishes to communicate. If reprinting an existing catalogue this might simply require updating product and service information so the design remains the same. However, if printing leaflets to support a sales promotion then the designer needs to understand the promotion objectives and the characteristics of the target audience.

If using a new designer or design team then provide them with existing printed materials that are good examples of the image that the organisation wishes to communicate. Organise the print job early enough to allow the designer to put forward initial ideas that can be developed to meet requirements. Prepare a plan that covers important timescales and deadlines including:

- Creative and print brief.
- Development of copy.
- Selection of pictures.
- Photography.
- Final design decision.
- Proofing.
- Printing.
- Delivery.
- Distribution.

Activity: 7.4: Creativity unleashed

Write a creative brief for an advertising campaign for a new chocolate bar aimed at the teenage market. Compare your ideas with fellow students or colleagues.

If possible ask the person in your organisation, or one you know well, to let you sit in on a meeting to brief designers at the start of an advertising campaign or similar.

Using pictures in printed materials

The advent of digital cameras means that good quality photographs can be produced and introduced into printed materials very quickly. Development time has been eliminated and the images can be sent electronically to the printer. Pictures and photographs are an effective way of representing products and services in brochures and catalogues.

Not only do images break up the text but they can also be used to simplify a complex message and demonstrate product use, size and features. In addition to pictures, symbols, icons, charts, graphs, diagrams, flow charts and signs are useful communication images. Including striking images also attracts attention and helps to make the printed material more memorable.

Designing effective printed materials

Consumers are bombarded with paper-based promotional materials, so leaflets, brochures and catalogues must be carefully designed to be attractive and easy to use. Consider the following:

- Present information clearly but concisely.

- Ensure sufficient white space so main messages are prominently displayed.

- For catalogues and brochures test out the design to see how easy they are to use.

- Avoid using lots of different sizes of print and font styles.

- Make good use of colour and ensure that the visual messages support rather than overpower. Remember, if there are severe budgetary constraints one colour does not have to be black and white, nor does two colour mean black plus one other. Experiment with different base colours that are 'company colours' such as dark blue. When using only two colours ensure there is a strong contrast such as dark blue and yellow, red or turquoise.

- Check grammar, spelling and punctuation.

- Check all contact details, product specifications, prices, promotional offers etc. are correct at the time of going to print and add a disclaimer to this effect if necessary.

Always proofread copy before it goes to print. Although you should ensure that you get a final proof – colour matched if appropriate (although there may be a charge for this) – it is easier to spot errors when looking at a black and white version of the copy. Once the final proof is signed off, you are responsible for mistakes in copy (even basic errors such as incorrect contact details), not the printer.

Remember when you are using copy or images that are not owned by your organisation to gain permission for doing so.

Activity 7.5: Design and print

Use a Gantt chart to plan the printing of a simple leaflet. The photographer needs 2 weeks to prepare photographs and the printer will take a week to print once the final proof has been signed off. The whole process must not take longer than 6 weeks.

Case Study – The International Conference Venue

The International Conference Venue (ICV) was built only ten years ago and features purpose-built conference/exhibition rooms, 200 bedrooms, dining and banqueting facilities plus the recently added sports and leisure centre.

Situated only one mile away from a major international airport, and with other excellent transport links, the ICV has become a well established and profitable business that has not had to try too hard to get its customers. Sales peak in the spring, while the venue is under-utilised in the summer, a common pattern in the industry.

For eight of its ten years' existence, the ICV was in the supreme position of being the only major venue within 50 kilometres of the airport, but two years ago Hilton opened a new hotel which included conference facilities. Three months ago, the Conference and Exhibition Centre (CEC) opened nearby and this poses a major threat.

Faced with new competition, the ICV built a new sports and leisure centre on-site. This features a swimming pool, saunas, comprehensive gymnasium, plus beauty and relaxation rooms. As yet, this has not proved as popular as had been hoped, despite the following packages being offered:

Day membership (for guests at the ICV)	£10
Day membership (for non-guests)	£15
Annual membership	£399
Corporate membership (up to 10 people)	£2,500

A possibility is that nearby residents and local companies either do not know of the leisure centre's existence or perceive it to be for guests staying at the ICV.

There are a number of different media options for advertising:

- *The Conferencer*, published monthly, reaches 20,000 decision makers in the industry. Rate £4,000 per page.

- *Conference Management*, a quarterly publication with a circulation of 10,000 senior executives. Rate £3,000 per page.

- *Events and Exhibitions*, a weekly publication, with a claimed readership of 50,000. Rate £5,000 per page.

- *Venue Selector*, a new publication mailed annually (January) to 100,000 business opinion formers. Rate £10,000 per page.

On past experience, 10% of the media budget has been set aside for advertising production.

Additionally a web design agency has quoted a price of £5,000 for a redesign of the site with monthly maintenance of £250.

Source: CIM Marketing in Practice examination paper, June 2001.

Questions

1. You have been given a budget of £55,000 and asked to produce a media plan for the next 6 months. It is now August. Justify your plan.

2. What recommendations can you make to increase summer usage? What media would you use?

3. What other media opportunities might you explore to raise awareness of ICV and its facilities?

SUMMARY OF KEY POINTS

- Marketers need to understand both customer and media characteristics if they are to be matched effectively.

- Criteria for media selection include cost, objectives of communication, ability to reach target audience and suitability.

- In advertising, burst campaigns are used to create a large impact and stimulate interest whereas drip campaigns are used to remind, when customers and consumers are already well informed.

- When preparing printed materials provide a creative brief to designers that includes purpose and message but also information about the organisation and its brands and values.

- Effective printed materials use colour and images to add interest. Use copy to give information but ensure it is clear and concise with lots of white space.

Improving and developing own learning

The following projects are designed to help you to develop your knowledge and skills further by carrying out some research yourself. Feedback is not provided for this type of learning because there are no 'answers' to be found, but you may wish to discuss your findings with colleagues and fellow students.

Project A

Visit the web site www.prsource.com and click on PR Newswire. Research the following:

i)   Writing a press release.

ii)   Writing a news article.

iii)   Using photographs to convey messages.

Use a Gantt chart to construct a planning schedule for the printing of a leaflet. You will need to include the following activities: preparing copy, photography, proofing copy, briefing photographer, printer and designer, final proofing before print, print time and delivery.

Project B

Collect a number of printed leaflets, catalogues and brochures to review the effectiveness of design, layout of information and use of colour.

What suggestions for improvements can you make? There are examples of printed materials throughout the core text: Dibb, Simkin, Pride and Ferrell, *Marketing Concepts and Strategies*, 2001.

Project C

Collect a number of printed leaflets, catalogues and brochures to review the effectiveness of design, layout of information and use of colour. What suggestions for improvements can you make? There are examples of printed materials throughout the core text: Dibb, Simkin, Pride, Ferrell, *Marketing Concepts and Strategies,* 2001.

Feedback on activities

Activity 7.1: Media merits

A table is a good way to summarise information, making it easier to draw comparisons.

Broadcast media	Benefits	Disadvantages
Television	■ Potential for accurate targeting. ■ Audience profiling information available. ■ Creative – sound, picture and movement. ■ High impact.	■ Cost. ■ Audience may not tune in.

Broadcast media	Benefits	Disadvantages
Cinema	■ Potential for accurate targeting. ■ Creative – sound, picture and movement. ■ High impact.	■ Cost. ■ Static audience.
Radio	■ Potential for accurate targeting. ■ Audience profiling information available. ■ Reasonable cost.	■ Limited creatively – sound only.

Print media	Benefits	Disadvantages
Newspaper	■ Potential for accurate targeting. ■ Audience profiling information available. ■ Potential for accurate targeting.	■ Cost. ■ Low impact. ■ Limited creatively – usually b&w.
Journal	■ Audience profiling information available. ■ Creative – colour, glossy medium.	■ Cost. ■ Low impact.
Poster	■ Cost-effective way of reaching a broad market. ■ Creative – colour and size. ■ High impact.	■ Limited potential for targeting. ■ Limited length of message possible.

Activity 7.2: Web alert!

What you should be looking for includes:

- The design of the home page and site map to help visitors identify what information and services are available.

- Ease and speed of navigation – is it easy to reach the pages required?

- Use of exciting copy and appropriate graphics.

- Ability for people to interact, respond and apply for further information.

- Added value of additional links.

- Consistent quality – the back pages should be as well designed as the front!

Activity 7.3: Fit to burst!

Your notes might be written as main points like a bulleted list:

- Multimedia, burst campaign required to cover the launch period including TV and glossy lifestyle magazines read by target audience.

- Drip campaign continued in glossies following launch period to act as a reinforcement.

- Use national and international TV and print media – review ability to reach target group.

- Review costs to determine duration of major activities – discuss the priority given to each media.

- Look at the recent figures relating to costs and discuss the duration of the drip campaign.

- Create a Duo web site to enhance the exclusivity of the product. Product must not be seen as a discounted product but discuss gift ideas, linking in with flowers and weekend breaks at exclusive country hotels.

- Customers enjoy being 'pampered' by salespeople so this product may not sell well on the Internet – discuss opportunities via large exclusive stores that increasingly wish to e-tail as well as retail.

- Review what use rival products make of the Internet.

- Discuss organising point of sale material for retail outlets to co-ordinate with media campaign and samples for personal salespeople.

- Discuss whether a celebrity couple can be used in the campaign – review costs and discuss this as a budget priority due to the product name.
- Review trade shows and select suitable event – may not be a priority.

From the above it can be appreciated that there are many opportunities for promotion of the product but priorities must be identified to guide decisions about how the budget should be spent. The objective might be to inform the consumer pre-launch and to raise awareness of the product and its benefits. Therefore, selecting a celebrity couple might be a top priority due to the name of the product and money might be allocated for this over and above extending the drip campaign. It also might be decided that the prime medium would be TV if the couple is seen frequently by the target group on television. Money would be allocated for this first and second to the print media. The results of previous campaigns would be scrutinised by the team to see what lessons could be learnt about spending money effectively and how to match media to objectives and target audience.

Activity: 7.4: Creativity unleashed

The creative brief would include the following information:

Client: Supertaste Sweets plc (background information enclosed).

Product: Superchoc bar (product development information enclosed).

Date: 01/09/02

Campaign: A 3 minute advertisement to appear four times during primetime television (6-9pm) for 4 weeks during November to support the launch of the new product.

Purpose: To generate awareness of a new product. To establish the brand within target market.

Target audience: Teenage market aged 11 to 18 years, young people at school and starting their first job.

Proposition: A bar of chocolate that can be shared with friends. Use group situations where teenagers can be seen having fun and enjoying bars of Superchoc together.

Brand image: Fun, easy to eat, easy to share.

Activity 7.5: Design and print

Task	Week 1	Week 2	Week 3	Week 4	Week 5	Week 6
Brief designer	■					
Organise copy	■					
Finalise design				■		
Proof copy			■			
Brief photographer	■					
Brief printer		■				
Final proof					■	
Print and deliver						■

Session 8

Product and place

Introduction

When developing the marketing plan, the Marketing Manager decides how to co-ordinate the four Ps so each element is supported by the other. This Session and the next looks at the four elements individually – product and place, price and promotion – but begins by considering the co-ordination of all four. Price and promotion are then examined in further detail.

In a competitive environment it is important for marketers to monitor customer needs and competitor activity and to identify product trends. This information is used to make adjustments in existing products so they continue to meet customer requirements and reflect changing consumer preferences. Organisations also need to look continuously for new ways to get their products in front of customers and consumers. The Internet represents new opportunities to do this but marketers must not overlook the more traditional channels.

This Session explores why marketers need to monitor product trends and the implications for tactical marketers of the PLC, how to evaluate the effectiveness of current channels of distribution and how to identify additional opportunities. Although the word 'product' is used throughout the Session, it includes services delivered either as part of the product or as the product itself.

LEARNING OUTCOMES

At the end of this Session you will be able to:

- Explain what is meant by co-ordinating the marketing mix.
- Describe how organisations monitor product trends.
- Explain why organisations need to develop new products.
- Discuss the marketing of products at different stages in the PLC.
- Describe the current distribution channels for an organisation and evaluate new opportunities.

Co-ordinating the four Ps

Price, Promotion, Product and Place, the four Ps, are not independent of each other. The features of a product are taken into account when making price decisions; the nature of a product is used to determine suitable distribution channels and so on. Effective marketing means co-ordinating the elements of the marketing mix because they are related and inter-dependent. In the next two Sessions each will be explored in turn to show examples of the different aspects of the relationship between the elements and how they fit in the mix.

Activity 8.1: A car that is driving success

Read the following article that appeared in *Marketing Business*, September 2000, and note examples of 'marketing mix co-ordination' for the Golf car.

The VW car sits in the lower medium A sector of the car market, which for many years has accounted for around one third of all new cars sold per year. In comparison to, for example, 4x4s or MPVs, it is a static sector of the market. The models sold are mass market hatchback cars, with men accounting for around 60% of purchases.

Volkswagen's Mark 4 Golf was launched in April 1998 with the brand positioning 'understanding refinement and engineering excellence.' 1998 was a dynamic year for car launches, also witnessing the introduction of the Ford Focus, the new Vauxhall Astra and the Citroën Xsara. Despite this fierce competition, volume targets for the new Golf were all achieved. Brand share during the year following the launch increased by 209% – from 3.3% to 10.2%. During the same period, other sector leaders saw a decline – with the exception of the Astra.

Volkswagen's advertising spend was a little less than Ford and Vauxhall during 1998, and substantially less than Ford in 1999.

£k advertising spend versus major competitors (all media)		
Model	**1998**	**Jan-May 1999**
Golf	£15,996	£5,735
Escort/Focus	£18,674	£12,005
Astra	£16,524	£3,492
Megane	£14,789	£2,560
Peugeot 306	£14,749	£3,982

Source: AC Nielsen Meal

According to a spokesperson for the company, the Golf's image and reputation improved to "leading levels" and committed demand increased to a point where "it became the most desirable car in this sector of the market".

What is a product?

A product is anything that is capable of fulfilling a customer need and may be tangible or intangible such as a service. Services are further defined in the next Session but it is important to note that the term product covers both. A product can also be a person, such as a celebrity or a place as well as a consumer or industrial good or service.

Consumer products are those that are produced for the benefit of consumers and their families. Industrial products are produced for organisations and sold to organisational buyers. The terms industrial buyers and business to business markets are also used in this context.

Products are produced to satisfy a basic customer need, so a car satisfies the need to travel independently – this is called the 'core' product. The actual product refers to the features that the product needs in order to satisfy a customer so, for a car, this would include standard safety features, comfortable seats, etc. The 'augmented' product includes the additional features that help differentiate rival products and includes the added value factors that customers will pay additional money for. In a car this represents the higher specification car which might include satellite navigation, metallic paint finish or extended warranty. Many products include some service elements and the quality of these might influence customer preference. Consumers may also select one brand over another because of the added value they perceive in that brand.

When developing new products or modifying existing ones to meet changing customer requirements, the other elements of the mix need to be considered – what price to charge, where to sell and how best to promote to the target audience. How these three Ps are combined will be different for each product. Modifications might be made to satisfy a new distribution opportunity so a mobile hairdresser will offer a different service compared to one working at a salon but there will be the benefit of convenience for the customer. However, the full range of services will not be available so pricing may need to reflect this. The cost base will also be different because there are no premises costs, but mobile equipment and a car are required.

New product development

New product development is a risky area for organisations because a high proportion of new products do not make it to market and therefore vast sums of money can be lost. Product failure can also be damaging to an organisation's reputation. However, if a breakthrough product is developed then high sales will be guaranteed. Examples of industries in which new product development has a significant role to play are manufacturers of IT equipment, mobile phones and pharmaceuticals. Consumers have high expectations of new, exciting products offering further benefits, although growth is slowing down in some areas due to the high cost of new products that do not provide benefits which hold a corresponding high value for potential users.

Therefore, unless the organisation has a reputation for research and development and the introduction of new products is a key factor in maintaining this image, it is better to look for alternative ways to increase sales or market share. This may mean looking for new market opportunities for the product (market development) or increasing the frequency of purchase through promotion or stressing an alternative use for the product to existing customers (market penetration).

Monitoring product trends

As previously discussed in Session 3, marketers need to gather data and information to inform decision making. Effective organisations continually research consumer preferences in their chosen markets and gather customer feedback to anticipate changing demands and requirements. Modifications can then be made to existing products to meet these to extend the life of the product. This is explored later in this Session.

In the consumer market food manufacturers constantly research changing consumer tastes and requirements to ensure product ranges continue to sell. Changing lifestyle preferences has led to many products modified to provide low fat alternatives and organic options. Car manufacturers have responded to consumer concerns and government influence by building in additional safety features to standard models. Publishers update text books and new magazines are introduced which cater for growing consumer passions such as healthy lifestyles.

Product, price and promotion need to be carefully integrated if product modifications are to be successful. The change may be a factor that customers expect as standard so will not be willing to pay a higher price. However, if it represents a further benefit then they will be willing to pay for the added value. Often, changes are promoted via new packaging supported by an advertising campaign and sales promotion. A quick look round your local supermarket will provide many examples of this.

In business to business markets sales representatives are a rich source of information about changing customer requirements because they have direct access to buyers and decision makers. Effective monitoring of product trends and development is a fine balance between responding to new requirements before the competition but also learning from the competition. Many manufacturers make core products that can be customised to meet individual customer specifications. If making mass market products then it is important to decide how much change is needed to update and be aware of how the competition is responding. If they can make the change at a lower cost, then it may be a time to exit that market and re-deploy resources where there is less risk.

Activity 8.2: Cleaning up!

Read the extract from a short article that appeared in *Marketing Business*, September 2000, and then answer the questions set:

Fabric washing detergents is a mature market, which had a retail value of around £900m in 1997. Lever Brothers and Procter & Gamble dominate the market, with an average share of about 15%. The two strongest brands are Persil and Arial.

Lever Brothers' introduction of Persil tablets was viewed as heralding the biggest revolution in the laundry sector for more than a decade. They were a totally new concept, developed in direct response to consumers' wishes for a more convenient washing product. Persil tablets gained almost 9% of the total market share value within 3 months of launch – a value of £6.6m per month.

Questions

1. Why do you think that this was such a success story?

2. How were the risks associated with new product development minimised?

The Product Life Cycle (PLC)

The PLC is based on the concept that a product has a life: birth (introduction) and death (decline). Many products now have a shorter life cycle because they are more likely to become obsolete due to new technology or effective competitor activity.

Figure 8.1 compares the main marketing implications for products at different stages of the life cycle.

Stage of the PLC	Marketing implications
Pre-launch.	■ No sales but high Research and Development (R&D) costs. ■ Piloting to survey consumer response prior to launch – this may also provide information for the launch advertising campaign. ■ Monitoring of potential competition; early launch might be indicated to beat a rival product to market. ■ Limited pre-launch promotion concentrating on informing.

Stage of the PLC	Marketing implications
Introduction.	■ Sales to innovators and early adopters so the product begins to make a return on investment, but it is unlikely that there will be profits. ■ Innovative products may attract high prices but this is an experimental stage for prices. ■ Few competitors. ■ Promotion is a high priority to build awareness, advertising to inform of benefits, PR activities to raise awareness among target groups and opinion leaders, sales promotion to incentivise, personal selling is very important. ■ Failure rate is high. ■ Distribution may be limited and highly targeted.
Growth.	■ Rapid sales leading to profit. ■ Increase in competition so profits may fall later in this stage. ■ Prices may be discounted to increase sales. ■ Promotion is concentrated on increasing sales and strengthening the brand, so may be a high level of sales promotion and advertising with PR support and sponsorship. Personal selling is still very important. ■ This stage is critical to product survival. ■ Distribution is widened.
Maturity.	■ Growth slows and starts to decline so profits are reduced, but still potential for strong brands. This depends on the level of sales promotion that is required to maintain the product and prevent decline. ■ Marketers are experienced at pricing. ■ Weaker competition is forced out as stronger products and brands survive.

Stage of the PLC	Marketing implications
Maturity (contd.)	■ High level of consumer knowledge so advertising may be focused on persuasion and reinforcement to enhance brand preference so may be an increase in PR activities and sponsorship. ■ Products may be further refined or augmented to meet changing needs if sales are to be sustained. ■ Distribution is maximised and new channels may be found to improve product visibility and increase sales.
Decline.	■ Follows saturation of the market, sales and profits are falling as new improved rival products take over. ■ Price may be discounted to get the last remaining sales. ■ Promotion may be continued to specific targeted groups or halted to reduce costs. ■ Distribution may be limited to cut costs and product deleted as customers decline rapidly.

Figure 8.1: Marketing implications for products at different stages of the life cycle

Marketers need to combine the elements of the marketing mix in different ways at each stage of the PLC to encourage growth and maintain market share. Once the product has been overtaken by substitutes and there is no 'life left' then it is deleted from the product portfolio. Some products survive relatively short periods of time because they were developed to cater for a specific fad or fashion but others may have long lifetimes if they can be modified or adapted to meet changing consumer needs and preferences.

Activity 8.3: Club cafés

Club cafés are typical of the pavement cafés found in many European and Mediterranean countries but are situated in up-market town centres in the UK. They attract shoppers and business people who call in typically for a coffee and snack during the day. Light lunches are also served. At present they are not open at night but are located well for this trade and plans are in the pipeline for this. However, since the launch of the chain twelve months ago trading has been disappointing and turnover is only half what was expected.

As Marketing Manager, draft a meeting agenda for the promotions team to look at how sales can be increased.

Place

As mentioned above, products need to be available to customers and consumers. The Internet and other developments in distribution have increased the 'place' opportunities which will be discussed later in the Session.

A producer can sell directly to the customer or use a channel for distribution that consists of a number of different intermediaries such as wholesalers, retailers and other agents such as dealers and distributors. Each intermediary in the chain normally buys the products to sell on to the next, so producers may use channel promotions to push products through the system.

Consider a simple marketing channel that consists of the producer, wholesaler, retailer and consumers.

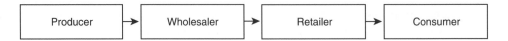

If employing a push strategy the producer would promote to wholesalers, the wholesalers to retailers and retailers to consumers. One channel member promotes to the next in-line. When using a pull strategy the producer promotes directly to the consumer in order to create strong demand so the retailers go to the wholesalers or producers.

Most companies use a combination of push and pull. Products are promoted directly to consumers via advertising, sales promotions and other communications, possibly via the company web site. In addition, trade advertising and personal selling, through company representatives, informs the channel members of the predicted consumer demand for the product. Timing is critical and the speed at which information can be transmitted electronically is a vital part of this process.

Technology has increased efficiency of distribution channels in terms of speed of transfer of data and information, but effective management is required to ensure that the right goods are dispatched to the right customer at the right time. Mistakes further up the channel have a knock-on effect all the way along to the customer.

Evaluating channel options

Producers need to make decision about which distribution option is best for them as an organisation, their product and the market. Factors that affect this decision include:

- Advantage of using intermediaries – producers can reduce money tied up in stock holding and minimise transport costs by using intermediaries. Logistic companies specialising in warehousing and distribution may be more efficient at this than producers and may be able to employ economies of scale if they distribute products for several manufacturers.

- Disadvantages of using intermediaries – each agent in the channel adds an additional cost and delays the product reaching the market.

- Control – producers may wish to retain control of distribution to ensure high levels of service.

- Competitors' activity – if they are finding new ways of reaching customers they may take market share, so producers must constantly evaluate effectiveness of their distribution.

- Customer preferences – changing lifestyles mean that customers may wish to change the method of accessing the product – e-commerce has developed because people wish to purchase a greater range of products via the Internet.

- New opportunities – new technology makes it easier for producers to reach customers via interactive television and the Internet.

New channels of distribution

The Internet has revolutionised distribution for many producers. Many companies took the opportunity of being the first to sell their products and services online.

Marketers could promote directly to the consumer – thus reducing costs – but products still had to be delivered to the consumer and this is the problem that many ran into. Poor management and lack of expertise led to late deliveries and disappointed customers and a rationalisation among online sellers.

A well-known success story in the e-commerce industry is book retailer Amazon.com which put customer service at the heart of their business. Many High Street names such as John Lewis combine e-tailing with retailing by carefully selecting which products to sell online.

Two major consumer factors still stifle growth in online shopping. One is security. Consumers are reluctant to use credit cards online and they still like to touch and feel many products before purchasing. However, many airlines are finding that customers increasingly prefer to book online rather than through an agent because of the significant cost savings that are available.

Telephone call centres are making an increasingly significant impact on many service distribution channels such as booking airline tickets, holiday reservations, insurance renewals and financial services.

M-commerce is also increasing the opportunity for producers to reach customers. Wireless Application Protocol (WAP) allows the customer access to the Internet so they can take advantage of e-commerce on the move! The disadvantage of this channel at present is the poor quality of image on screen and the slowdown in growth of the mobile phone market.

Activity 8.4: Marketing magic – Harry Potter

Read the following extract from the article that appeared in Marketing Business, November 2001, and answer the questions set:

Bloomsbury Publishing launched J. K. Rowling's Harry Potter and the Goblet of Fire to the world's press by hiring a steam train, painting it in the colours of the Hogwarts Express (the train from the stories) and stationing it at King's Cross, London. After the launch it travelled around the country making eight stops and meeting hundreds of fans along the way. J. K. Rowling signed thousands of books and the stunt received coverage all over the world and across all media.

Harry Potter and the Goblet of Fire has exceeded its target sales and the Harry Potter series now accounts for 19.1% of total children's book sales, compared to 3.9% for the next best-selling series.

Questions

1. What might limit Internet opportunities from a legal point of view?

2. What makes the Internet an ideal place for publishers to sell books?

Case Study – Brave new ideas

Problem: you have a product that is a clear world-beater, but your sales team is not selling as well as they might. What do you do? You may be tempted to blame the marketing strategy or fire the sales team.

But, if the problem is anything like that faced by Eyretel, the fast-growth, high-tech start-up that sells recording and data equipment for call centres, the answer may be neither.

Eyretel found the solution lay in innovating its sales process. Its product is packed with enough technical wizardry to baffle the brains of a fully paid-up nerd. And it is marketed in the highly regulated telecommunications industry where breaking the rules can carry a hefty fine.

Both made the equipment a complex sell. And as Eyretel was growing at stratospheric rates, it was nearly impossible to recruit enough salespeople who combined technical know-how with industry knowledge. The company solved the problem by taking a hard look at what happened from the time it received an order to the moment it booked the order.

Its key problem was that the range of configurations was so large, customers needed a salesperson's help to guide them to the right choice. Trouble was, not all salespeople had enough technical knowledge to do that. So often a technical specialist would have to accompany them on sales calls. Expensive for Eyretel and not impressive from the customer's point of view.

Eyretel solved the problem by analysing the sales process, collecting best practice knowledge from the firm's most effective salespeople and technicians and codifying it all in an 'expert system' – essentially, a knowledge database. Now salespeople take a laptop computer loaded with the system – rather than a technician – to customer meetings. They use the laptop to give the customer a presentation and then take the order.

Stage by stage the expert system helps the salesperson collect all the information that is needed to define the best configuration for the customer. A red traffic light shows on the screen until all the information needed at that stage has been entered correctly. Then it turns to green and the salesperson and the customer move on to the next step. At the end the system automatically prices the proposed configuration – another earlier source of errors.

This bright idea has had a big impact on Eyretel's ration of sales to support staff. The firm doesn't need so many people in the back office compiling presentations, drafting proposals and costing orders. And, as a bonus, within days of the system going live, one salesman took an order which paid for the development process.

Source: *Marketing Business*, October 2001.

Questions

1. What was the main benefit that Eyretel achieved by innovating the sales process?

2. Why do you think that sales representatives represent an effective way of reaching customers?

3. What other channel of distribution might they use in the future?

SUMMARY OF KEY POINTS

- New product development is essential as products become obsolete and the consumer needs change or development, but it holds a high risk factor.

- Being the first to market with an innovative product that meets consumer expectations is key to gaining market share and high sales.

- Products need to be promoted in different ways during each stage of the PLC.

- Many organisations are not able to sell directly to the end-user so employ channel intermediaries with specific skills and expertise to help distribute their products.

- The rapid pace of the development of new technologies, including digital technologies, has opened up many opportunities for organisations to reach their customer and restructure existing distribution channels.

Improving and developing own learning

The following projects are designed to help you to develop your knowledge and skills further by carrying out some research yourself. Feedback is not provided for this type of learning because there are no 'answers' to be found, but you may wish to discuss your findings with colleagues and fellow students.

Project A

Review the products and services that you use on a regular basis.

How have they been modified or changed over recent years?

What further trends will drive further developments in the near future?

Project B

Identify two products at the growth stage of their life cycle, one of which is growing fast and one of which is not.

Why do you think this happening?

As a marketer what would you do next?

Project C

Visit www.amazon.co.uk and www.1800flowers.com and make notes on the effectiveness of each as a distribution channel for the organisation.

Feedback on activities

Activity 8.1: A car that is driving success

In the lead-up to the product launch, advertising has raised awareness of the product among consumers and has contributed to branding activities. It is interesting to note that although Volkswagen's advertising spend was less than Ford's, the product appeared to be more successful, perhaps indicating that the marketing mix was co-ordinated more effectively – or that the Golf advertising campaign was more effective. It is difficult to measure the exact contribution of each element due to the inter-dependence of one element on another.

Other elements that might have contributed to the success of the Golf might include strong news releases, targeted sales promotions, well-trained and informed salespeople at retail outlets and other events designed to strengthen and support brand positioning.

Activity 8.2: Cleaning up!

1. Persil tablets were the first to market and offered a solution to consumers' desire for convenience.

2. The extract suggests that consumer research had been analysed to identify what was needed and that need was met promptly and effectively.

Activity 8.3: Club cafés

AGENDA

To: A. Brown
       C. Dowd
       E. French
       (Promotions Team)

From: T. Thomas
        Marketing Manager
        Email: tthomas@marketingplus.com

Date: 20th October 2002

Meeting: The next meeting of the promotions team will take place on 5th November. The purpose is to review the first twelve months trading of the Club cafés and identify ways of increasing sales in the immediate future. The growth of sales has been disappointing and it is a priority for improvement as competition is fierce. Café locations have been reviewed and are ideal for the target group. Please look at the following agenda and let me have any points you want added by 31st October in time for circulation 2 days prior to our meeting. The meeting will begin at 2pm and end promptly at 4pm.

1.	Apologies for absence	TT
2.	Minutes of last meeting	TT
3.	Review of marketing support following launch and lessons learnt	TT
4.	Financial report	TT
5.	Options for sales promotions (team brainstorm)	All
6.	Options for other marketing support	All
7.	Review of brand development	TT
8.	Action planning	TT
9.	AOB	All
10.	Date of next meeting	TT

Activity 8.4: Marketing magic – Harry Potter

1. Copyright is always a consideration for marketers wishing to take opportunities offered by electronic media to reach target audiences and wider groups. Owning rights to print media does not mean that the same information can be used on the Internet – separate permission must be sought for digital rights. Bloomsbury has created a web site and online Harry Potter club but activities are limited because Warner controls the digital rights to the series.

2. Amazon.com is a well-known example. Customers find it quick and convenient to purchase online. In addition incentives such as sample chapters can be given away to encourage purchase.

Session 9

Price and promotion

Introduction

The pricing of a product is a complex decision depending on a number of internal and external factors, so these are discussed in this Session. The different activities that make up what is called the promotional mix are evaluated to help marketers make decisions about effectiveness of each in different situations. Although the word product is used throughout the Session it also includes services.

LEARNING OUTCOMES

At the end of this Session you will be able to:

- Analyse the impact of pricing decisions and the role of price within the marketing mix.

- Evaluate promotional activities and opportunities including sales promotion, PR and collaborative programmes.

Pricing decisions

As part of the marketing mix, pricing strategies are only effective if they are consistent with those made for the other elements, promotion, product and place.

Consider the following two examples:

- Budget retailers usually rely on a limited range of product lines so they can concentrate on offering the lowest prices. Stores are minimalist and all other aspects of marketing are designed to be as inexpensive as possible. Shoppers self-select and do not expect to be pampered! Outlets will be located in areas that have the highest footfall of shoppers for whom low price is a major criterion for purchase. Online or mail order catalogue is also a cost-effective means of reaching price-conscious consumers.

- Designer clothes are presented to shoppers in a different way with personal sales assistants ready to assist customers in every way possible. Designer labels are sold in the most 'fashionable' locations with every comfort afforded to shoppers such as coffee, sofas to relax on and spacious fitting rooms. Décor is luxurious to match the product and if sold in large stores, designer lines are often located on a different floor from lower-priced clothes. Manufacturers will supply high quality merchandising material and keep a tight control on how it is used to protect and strengthen their brand. Prices are higher than non-designer labels because of the added value of the designer name which customers are willing to pay for.

From the above it can be appreciated that there are a number of influences on product pricing decisions as shown below:

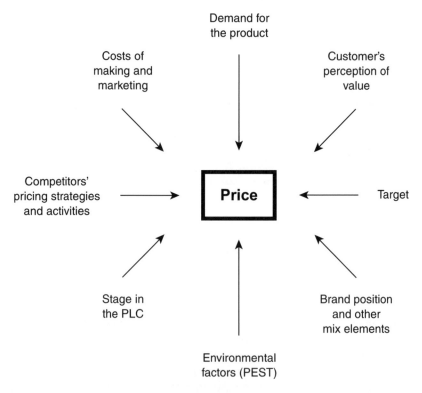

Figure 9.1: Factors that influence pricing decisions

Some of these factors are external, such as demand for the product and competitors' pricing strategies, whereas costs are internal. The position of the product in its life cycle is also significant and this will be explored later in this Session.

Pricing strategies

The two main strategies used by marketers are:

- **Skimming**

  Prices are higher to attract the least price sensitive customer segment – 'skimming the cream off the market'. This is possible where demand is high and there is little competition. Examples include new products that include the latest technological developments such as computers, mobile phones and televisions. Once this segment is satisfied, prices must be reduced to develop sales in other customer groups. The exception is products that are niche marketed – demand is limited by high price to maintain exclusivity.

  The advantage of this strategy, particularly for new products, is the opportunity to make high profits before competitors introduce substitute products. A main disadvantage may be that sales are limited and rivals are attracted into the market by the opportunity to sell at high prices.

- **Penetration**

  Prices are lower in order to attract as many target customer groups as possible – penetrating the market. A low price strategy may be used to stimulate demand where this has fallen, or to push other competitors who cannot match the low price out of the market. If companies find new, cheaper ways to produce products they have an opportunity to be a price leader and suffocate weaker rivals.

  The advantages also include faster growth in sales and a larger customer base but profits may be reduced and customers may not continue to buy if it becomes necessary to put the price up later.

Price wars

Price wars are increasingly common in today's competitive environment. Marketers are aware of consumer fatigue on the high street due to constant sales and in business to business markets sales representatives constantly have to negotiate lower prices or offer additional incentives to retain a customer.

Companies reduce prices temporarily or permanently to:

- Counteract a slow down in demand.
- Increase market share.

- Boost sales.
- Gain competitive advantage.

Lowering prices means reducing profits although the volume of sales increases. In order to offer lower price, companies may be forced to cut costs and risk compromising the level of service offered or even product quality. If clothing manufacturers use an inferior material to reduce costs and prices they risk alienating existing customers who have come to expect a certain standard of durability in the product and attract lower spending customers who are likely to be lost if prices are raised. However, if the objective is to increase the customer base, reducing prices to stimulate demand may be an effective option.

Activity 9.1: Price wars

You have been asked to give a short presentation to marketing students on the potential impact on organisations of price wars and the potential long-term effects.

Prepare two slides to highlight the main points you wish to communicate.

The promotional mix

The promotional mix comprises advertising, sponsorship, PR, sales promotion and personal selling. When deciding how much of each element to use, the marketer must consider the mix as a whole as each activity will impact on the others. Communications must be consistent. For example, when building a brand, activities must be co-ordinated and designed to reinforce the main advantages of that brand over competitor products. An advertising campaign may be scheduled to support a sales promotion and front-line salespeople.

Each element of the promotional mix is explored separately.

Sales promotion

Successful sales promotions increase sales for the lifetime of the promotion. The effect is immediate and not usually sustained significantly once it has ended because the incentive to buy has been removed.

Common incentives offered include free gift, money off, discounted price, more for the same price and two for one or three for two. There are a number of factors that marketers need to consider when planning a sales promotion:

Dimensions	Factors
Objectives.	By how much do sales need to be increased, over what period of time?
Target market.	Why do consumers need an additional incentive to purchase?
Incentive.	How much? If competitors are already discounting heavily the decision for the marketer is whether to undercut or consider another form of promotion.
Duration.	How long will it take for consumers to respond? Can it be extended at short notice if necessary?
Timing.	What else is happening? Seasonal sales? Integration with other elements of the promotional mix.
Promotional mix.	How should it be integrated with other mix elements?
Competitors.	What are they doing, planning to do or have done in the recent past?
Budget.	What will it cost?
Pre-testing.	Should this be done to determine potential response?
Legal issues.	Is the promotion legal? For example, are the offers available to all that are eligible?
Evaluation.	Evaluation. What are the measures of effectiveness? (Usually increase in sales).
Marketing support material.	What is required? By when?
Training.	Do salespeople need training?

Figure 9.2: Factors to consider when planning sales promotions

Promotions may be planned far in advance to support the growth of a new product or at relatively short notice if sales begin to drop. Manufacturers will often work together with retailers or other intermediaries in the distribution chain to help push products. This may include free display material for stores, contribution towards direct mail costs, sale or return facilities to encourage stores to hold additional stock, free staff training and sales force competitions. Sharing the cost of a promotion reduces the costs and, if skillfully handled, should meet the objectives of both organisations.

Activity 9.2: Increasing sales

The marketing manager of a publishing house has asked you to help her explore ways of increasing sales through the company web site.

What suggestions can you make?

Advertising

In contrast to sales promotions, this element is designed to have a longer-term effect and is used to inform, persuade and reinforce. When new products are introduced the objective of the pre-launch advertising may be to inform consumers of the new product and its features and benefits. Later in its life cycle, advertising may be used to persuade them to purchase or remain loyal to the brand. Later in the growth phase or at maturity the decision may be taken to use advertisements to reinforce previous messages to reassure customers that they have made the right decision to buy.

To be effective, the advertisement must create the desire within the consumer to purchase. All advertisements need to attract attention but the way they do this will be different according to the objective of the campaign. If reinforcing or persuading, a subtle approach might be adopted whereas if informing them, some element of factual benefit must be incorporated. Advertising is employed to increase sales but not reduce profit, although it can be used to inform consumers about a sales promotion.

Examples of effective campaigns are numerous. Many consumers remember the PG Tips chimps on television enjoying cups of tea. Early in 2002, it was announced that the chimps will no longer be used to advertise PG Tips tea but they will be remembered with affection by many when the new campaign is released, illustrating how long the effect of a popular campaign can last.

In contrast to sales promotions, marketers can use dynamic media such as television and cinema for advertising. However, it is difficult to personalise the message, whereas sales promotions can be targeted to individuals through direct mailing or email.

In the print media, advertising is charged by the space taken. If you are responsible for this it is often possible to negotiate a discount on standard rates if you are booking a series of advertisements. If you have a good relationship with the advertising editor and their department, they might offer you heavily discounted space at short notice if bookings are low for one publication.

Measuring the effectiveness of advertising is difficult unless a coupon is used. Many organisations survey customers to find out how they heard of the organisation or what influence advertising had on their decision to, but this is not very reliable as customers may not remember or even reply truthfully, not wishing to acknowledge that they responded to the pressure of advertising! Increase in sales, sales leads and market share are common measures but it is difficult to isolate the exact contribution of advertising as many sales campaigns use an integrated approach.

In order to test the effectiveness of communication, advertisers may pre-test by showing it to a group of target consumers and gathering feedback. Alternatively, they may test recall immediately following the campaign by surveying consumers about which advertisements they can remember seeing recently.

Activity 9.3: Misleading consumers

There are many authorities and professional bodies that set codes of practice for members to adhere to. Examples include the Independent Television Commission and the Radio Authority in the UK.

Write some brief notes on why codes of practice are necessary.

Public relations

The definition of PR from the Institute of Public Relations is:

'The deliberate, planned and sustained effort to establish and maintain mutual understanding between an organisation and its publics'.

The organisation's PR activities are designed to communicate positive messages to its publics that help develop image, reputation and brand. They may also be used to respond to a crisis or to negative publicity, sometimes called 'damage limitation' exercises.

The main publics of an organisation are derived from the following groups:

- Consumers, customers and users.
- Suppliers.
- Distributors.
- Opinion leaders.
- Finance sector.
- Local community.
- Employees.
- Potential employees.
- Trades Unions.
- Media.

The objectives of different communications may include to change attitudes of target groups such as users or opinion leaders who influence others, or to improve relationships with employees or the local community. Matching media to PR activities is dependent upon the ability to reach the target audience and many campaigns use a multimedia approach to gain widespread coverage. The marketer working in PR uses numerous opportunities to communicate, both internally and externally, including news releases, interviews, VIP visits, open days and speeches given by key personnel.

The following examples illustrate the range of PR activities that may be undertaken:

- The PR manager has a significant role to play in facilitating good community relations. Supermarkets listen to local concerns when applying for planning permission for a new site. They often face opposition from local pressure groups so they may attempt to counter this by providing additional local facilities, such as a community centre, or landscaping the surrounding area. A caring, positive image may help with staff recruitment because more local people are encouraged to apply for vacancies once the supermarket is built.
- News releases to announce creation of new jobs, product launch, sponsorship deal, productivity or people management award, new customer benefits etc.

These need to be targeted to specific print and broadcast editors, either local or national as appropriate.

- Co-ordinating and reviewing the content of the annual report and Chief Executive's speech to be given at the annual shareholders' meeting and posted on the company web site.

- Producing press packs for exhibitions, press conferences and outlet launches.

- Overseeing publication of the in-house newsletter for all employees.

Sponsorship

There are several major benefits that organisations look for when considering sponsorship deals:

- The opportunity for widespread exposure of the corporate name and brand to target audiences, local, national and global. Large events attract high-level sponsors whose name is then broadcast to television viewers, radio listeners and photographed by the press media. TV sponsorship is also common whereby manufacturers associate their products with a particular television series because the programme is viewed by target groups.

- Opportunity to develop positive attitudes towards brands so manufacturers of sports equipment, cars and health care products sponsor appropriate exciting spectator sports and popular events.

- Internal employee motivation. Many organisations believe that their employees are proud to see their company associated with a high profile event or person, particularly if it is a worthy cause or activity.

Marketers working on any element of the promotional mix are becoming increasingly creative in their approach to try to attract attention, and sponsorship is no exception. Therefore, almost any object, person or event might attract sponsorship.

The key questions that the sponsor must ask before entering into an agreement with another party are:

- What is the potential for exposure to target audience?
- Is the recipient of the sponsorship recognised by the target audience?
- Is the recipient of the sponsorship acceptable to the target audience?
- Does the sponsorship pose a threat to the corporate image or brand?
- For what period of time should sponsorship be given?

Clearly where there is little opportunity to be 'seen' by the target audience, or the activity may contain elements that might be considered controversial or unethical by the target audience, there is no real benefit in sponsorship. It is a difficult activity to evaluate in terms of return on investment, so the best opportunities are those that offer maximum exposure and minimum risk to brand or reputation.

Activity 9.4: Marketing Cinderellas

Read the extract from the article that appeared in *Marketing Business*, July/August 2000, and answer the questions set.

Maureen Taylor, Director of Leisure for the London Borough of Hackney found herself having to deal with a situation where the Borough (product) had attracted national notoriety. She was promoting the area when the tabloids ran a story about a local teacher who banned children from studying *Romeo and Juliet* by William Shakespeare because it "promoted heterosexual relationships". According to Taylor, "it was all blown up out of proportion but I decided to face the press head-on and turn a bad situation to our advantage."

She started a campaign to promote Hackney's historic connections with Shakespeare and persuaded the famous actor and gay rights supporter, Sir Ian McKellen, to unveil a plaque to Shakespeare, whose mentor Richard Burbage had a theatre in Shoreditch. "We got acres of free publicity including a double-page spread in *The Sun* newspaper," she recalls.

"When we promoted East London for Tourism and Investment we concentrated on the diverse ethnic mix, the historic treasures and the artistic vibrancy of the place," she summarises.

Questions

1. Why do you think the tactics used by Maureen Taylor to counter negative publicity about the London Borough of Hackney were successful?

2. What other ideas might you suggest? Brainstorm this with other students or colleagues to see how many creative ideas you can come up with.

Evaluating the elements of the promotional mix

The table below compares some different dimensions of the mix elements. How these are co-ordinated and integrated will depend on a number of factors, such as marketing objectives, budget and opportunity. However, it is useful to consider the merits of each to help marketers decide the potential for each tool in different situations.

Promotional element	Main objective	Media	Effect	Cost
Sales promotion.	To increase sales.	Print, Electronic.	Short term.	High but can be individually targeted.
Advertising.	To inform, persuade, reinforce.	Print, Broadcast, Electronic.	Long term, may be used to reinforce brand preference and encourage loyalty.	High but can be targeted to specific segments to increase effectiveness; discounts may be negotiated.
Publicity.	To inform, communicate positives, counteract negative messages.	Print, Broadcast, Electronic.	May be short, medium or long but continuous.	Medium to relatively low, can be targeted to specific segments.
Sponsorship.	To build and develop image and brand.	Print, Broadcast, Electronic.	Long term.	Medium to relatively low, can be targeted to specific segments.

Promotional element	Main objective	Media	Effect	Cost
Personal selling.	To sell, develop loyalty, build relationships.	Face to face.	Short term plus.	High due to one-to-one relationship with customer.

Figure 9.3: Summarising the merits of the promotional mix elements

Case Study – Giving is good business

The spotlight on Corporate Social Responsibility (CSR) is intense. After the 11th September 2001 terrorist attacks in America, and in the face of high profile anti-globalisation protests directed at corporations, the desire for a more socially responsible image has taken on a new urgency.

A recent survey by the *Guardian* newspaper found that the percentage of profits donated to charitable causes by UK companies was less than half that donated by their US counterparts. On average, FTSE 100 companies gave away 0.04 per cent of pre-tax profits, compared to 0.09 per cent by equivalent US firms.

Those UK companies that give more than the average – in some cases over 5 per cent of pre-tax profits – often stress the importance of community involvement as part of a socially responsible and cohesive corporate image that satisfies all stakeholders – employees, customers and shareholders – in equal measures.

They say Human Resources must expand the boundaries and work with Marketing to pave the way for a successful 'corporate story'.

In 2000 Royal & Sun Alliance Insurance Group gave away £3.5m. At 6.4 per cent of its pre-tax profits, this made it easily the most generous FTSE 100 company. John Hymers, UK Marketing Services Manager, explained why the group had launched a sponsorship scheme. This was aimed at helping young disaffected adults, who he said were often responsible for graffiti, housebreaking and other anti-social acts that led to claims ultimately paid for by the company.

"It is good business sense, not simply philanthropy," Hymers said, "It is part of an overall corporate marketing strategy. But the community as a whole benefits. We call it a three-way win. The community wins, the company benefits and the staff win."

For example, employees were given the opportunity to gain experience as coaches and administrators for sports events organised by the company.

"We present them with the initiatives and opportunities, largely through our company Intranet, and they respond," Hymers said. "There is a lot of encouragement from the top."

The community sponsorship scheme had a positive effect on new recruits as well as in the marketplace. "All stakeholders look to see what community involvement you have," he added.

Source: Originally published in *People Management*, 22nd November 2001 and reproduced with permission.

Questions

1. What is the full range of benefits that the Royal & Sun Alliance Insurance Group expect to gain from community sponsorship?

2. What might that the Royal & Sun Alliance Insurance Group do next to further communicate their sense of social responsibility?

3. Why is sponsorship a good way of promoting brand image?

SUMMARY OF KEY POINTS

- The 4 Ps need to be co-ordinated effectively by organisations to take advantage of the strengths offered by each element and their ability to support each other.

- Pricing decisions for products and services are influenced by many internal and external factors including PLC stage.

- Price has a strong impact on consumers' desire to buy – sales promotions that offer discounts and other incentives can be used to increase sales in the short term.

- The elements of the promotional mix each offer different opportunities for organisations to communicate with customers and consumers so should be co-ordinated to support and enhance the message. Consistency of communication is essential in order to build and develop brand and company image and reputation.

- Advertising is used to inform, influence or persuade.

- Sales promotions are used to increase sales in the short term.

- Sponsorship and publicity are used to raise awareness of brand and organisation.

- Personal selling offers organisations the ideal opportunity to meet specific customer requirements and is widely used in the b2b market.

Improving and developing own learning

The following projects are designed to help you to develop your knowledge and skills further by carrying out some research yourself. Feedback is not provided for this type of learning because there are no 'answers' to be found, but you may wish to discuss your findings with colleagues and fellow students.

Project A

Mobile phone companies have been criticised in the past because the pricing of units and services is complex and causes much confusion for consumers.

Do some research on the Internet to investigate how the industry is responding to such criticism.

You may wish to start by searching the archives at www.ft.com and www.thetimes.co.uk

Project B

Obtain the rate cards from a number of publications that your organisation uses regularly for advertising and calculate the cost of a full-page advertisement in full colour.

What are the differences in costs?

Why might you decide not to use the lowest cost publication?

If you can, discuss how advertising space is booked and the level of discount obtained.

Project C

Look for examples of promotions in different industry sectors such as Fast Moving Consumer Goods (FMCG), entertainment, hotel and catering, cars, holidays and others that interest you.

How do they differ?

Why might that be?

How effective is each at reaching its target groups?

Feedback on activities

Activity 9.1: Price wars

The main points to include are:

Potential impact on organisations
- Increased sales.
- Reduced profit.
- Enforced cost cutting.
- Conflict between quality and volume.
- Loss of loyal customers.

Possible long-term effects

- Reduced competition.

- Reduced choice for consumers.

- Impact on related markets.

- Difficult to end.

- Damage to 'quality' reputation.

Activity 9.2: Increasing sales

Sampling is a very effective promotional tool to use on the Internet. Free extracts or chapters can be provided for customers to download free as incentives to purchase a specific book. Having purchased, they could then be emailed with offers on other publications by the same author or ones that write similarly in the same genre.

Alternatively, customers can be offered a free download when they make a purchase. If this is a chapter from an award winning book or a very popular author it should be a powerful incentive.

Activity 9.3: Misleading consumers

Codes of practice provide guidelines for marketers and protection for consumers and marketers. When making decisions on how to use advertising, marketers need to be able to determine what messages can and cannot be used. Causing offence might create impact but it will attract the wrong kind of attention. Consumers need protecting, particularly children from offence, but they also need to be confident that claims made in advertisements are honest. Consumer confidence is essential if advertising is to be a powerful promotional tool for marketers.

Activity 9.4: Marketing Cinderellas

1. This was an example of a scare story which was based on scanty research – a media reaction rather than a balanced and reasoned piece of editorial. In this situation it was a sound decision to counter-attack because there was obviously lots of ammunition on Maureen Taylor's side. It is not always the best course of action because the other side may come back with more negative

publicity that attracts even more attention. This worked because it was based on fact and not exaggerated.

2. The campaign concentrated on the diverse ethnic mix, historic treasures and artistic vibrancy which are obviously strengths of the area. Making more of these through carnivals and events which featured well-known and popular celebrities, would enhance this image. Other ideas might include anything from half-marathons or fun runs around the area, art exhibitions to launch local artists, involving school children in street painting etc. – the list is endless!

Session 10

The extended marketing mix

Introduction

The extended mix was developed originally to market services but many products today also include an element of service so the 7Ps can also be applied equally to products. The importance of the three additional Ps – people, physical evidence and process – will be examined in this Session together with developments in information and communication technology which have implications for the marketing of services.

> ## LEARNING OUTCOMES
>
> At the end of this Session you will be able to:
>
> ■ Explain the importance of the extended marketing mix: how process, physical aspects and people affect customer choice.
>
> ■ Explain the importance of ICT in the new mix.

Service characteristics

The special characteristics of services have implications for marketers as discussed in Figure 10.1.

Service characteristic	Marketing implications
Intangibility.	A service cannot be touched and inspected in the same way that a product can be examined, so judgement of quality is subjective, based on personal feelings. For one person the attention received at a restaurant from a waiter will make the occasion special while another may find it overwhelming and intrusive.
Inseparability.	Services are consumed at the time of provision which has a significant impact on distribution. The Internet has increased the ability of organisations to provide services for consumers at a time and place that is convenient for them.

Service characteristic	Marketing implications
Heterogeneity.	Standardisation is difficult to achieve in services as the delivery may vary each time so each customer's experience may be different; whereas products can be produce to identical specifications. Value-added factors may be variably provided!
Perishability.	Services cannot be stored. Unlike manufacturers who can plan for sales promotions by buying additional stock, service providers need to be able to cope with demand at the time or 'lose the sale'.
Ownership.	Customers do not own a service in the same way as they can permanently own a product. Product demonstration must involve the consumer in the experience!

Figure 10.1: Service characteristics

Products and service are very different in terms of production and consumption. It is much easier to ensure the consistency of product quality because the same product can be manufactured in exactly the same way, to the same specifications and using the same raw materials. In addition, those that do not meet specification can be rejected before going to the customer, thus preventing dissatisfaction.

A service is consumed at the point of delivery so there is only one opportunity to get it right. Consistency cannot be guaranteed because of the human factor. Although it may always meet the required standard, the service might differ each time. The more standardised the service process and procedures, the easier it is to make it consistent.

Activity 10.1: Fast food fact finding

Do some research amongst your fellow students and colleagues on their experience of a local fast food restaurant.

Compare experiences.

How similar were they?

What were the differences?

How did these impact on your decision to return or recommend the restaurant?

Marketing services

From the above it can be appreciated that there are specific problems relating to the marketing of services. Unlike products, a service cannot be seen and so is difficult to promote – the consumer benefits from the effects of the service and enjoyment of the experience rather than the permanent ownership of a tangible object. Therefore, the marketer needs to identify what these are when advertising services and planning sales promotions. For example, a taxi firm might emphasise reliability and speed of response.

When marketing services it is common practice to promote the skill and the expertise of the people providing the service and the quality aspects of that service – speed, convenience etc. A solicitor's practice would include qualifications on the nameplates outside the practice, so that potential customers can see how well qualified they are to provide the service.

Testimony from previous clients is also used to gain client confidence and persuade them to try the service, but permission is required from the original source. This is similar to the marketing of products where recommendation might be used.

It is just as important to get the right mix when marketing services as it is for products. McDonald's would not satisfy customers if they were kept waiting for their meals, despite the friendly service and comfortable chairs. Quality of service is just as important as product quality.

Activity 10.2: Press release

Write a press release giving details of the opening of a new restaurant by a celebrity chef. Let your imagination go wild but remember it must be newsworthy!

---

3 extra Ps

To cover the different characteristics of services the marketed mix is extended to include three additional Ps – People, Process and Physical Evidence.

- People – the knowledge, skills, experience and attitudes required by the service providers and deliverers are key to ensuring the quality of service required. Customer loyalty may depend on the people, not only to provide a consistently good service but it may be the individual that is the key to individual customer retention. A customer may request to have their eyes tested by a named optician or deal with one particular salesperson at a car dealership. Seeing the same person means that they receive the 'same' service each time.

  Taking people out of the service reduces cost and delays. Many travel agents encourage consumers to use touch screen televisions to browse through holiday options and select preferred destinations before seeing a sales agent. The London Underground uses self-service ticket dispensers and some car parks allow customers to pay by swiping their credit card through a computerised system at the exit barrier.

- Process – computerised technology and automated systems has made some services more efficient but less personal. The advantage is that cost savings can be passed onto the customer making one service more competitive in price if it can be produced more cheaply than competitors. Some organisations provide services with different pricing structures according to the process involved, so customers may receive a discount for paying for utility services by direct debit rather than quarterly billing.

  Innovating processes can be the key to gaining competitive advantage, through lower cost or greater efficiency which is valued by the customer. Better processes lead to greater customer satisfaction and hopefully loyalty and recommendation.

- Physical evidence – the tangible dimension of the service! Includes the paperwork that accompanies ordering, billing, guarantees and warranties etc.

If these are user-friendly, then customers will tend to be more confident about the service. Complexity can cause confusion and lead to dissatisfaction and suspicion.

Other physical evidence includes premises where the service is consumed, appearance of staff and sales material. If a consumer is provided with a torn sales brochure by an untidy member of staff, he or she is likely to reject the service. All staff must be appropriately dressed to provide the service as well as friendly, well-informed about the service options and helpful. Appearance of premises, people and printed materials often count for first impressions, so must be right.

The company web site is another important feature of a service. It must be easy to navigate so the customer can locate the information required and complete all transactions quickly and efficiently. If a brochure is requested online then, if not electronically delivered, it must be posted out the same day. All processes must be efficient because each point of contact the customer has with an organisation makes a significant contribution to the overall level of satisfaction.

Activity 10.3: Misleading claims

As marketing manager of a transport company you pride yourself on the efficient service offered to customers. However, due to industrial disputes over pay, your services have recently deteriorated to the point that you have received widespread negative publicity in the local press and been branded as inefficient.

Unfortunately, on your advice, the company's recent recruitment advertisements focus on the efficient service you provide because you feel it is important to recruit people who are customer-focused. A number of people have complained to your customer care department that the advertisement is misleading. Write a memo to the HR Manager advising on what should be done.

The role of ICT in the new mix

As previously discussed, ICT has enhanced the ability or marketers to communicate with target groups and extend the provision of services to 24/7. In addition, new technology has also led to efficiencies in process, which can mean cost reduction and greater efficiency for customers.

Effective web sites can allow dialogue between customer and supplier. For example, customers of Fedex can track the progress of consignments via the company web site by entering a consignment number. The Internet can also be used to create virtual supply chains. Small distributors can enter orders to producers online, check stock levels and track order progress so they can give up-to-date information to customers at a click!

ICT has a significant impact on the marketing mix and can afford technically advanced organisations the opportunity to gain competitive advantage. However, where systems have replaced people, there may be disadvantages if consumers cannot access the information that would be provided by that person. In addition, many people are still not confident with online security, restricting the growth in e-tailing.

There are many examples of ICT improving the provision of services. Some that you may be familiar with are:

- Automated cash machines at banks so you are able to withdraw cash 24/7.

- Internet banking so you can check your accounts, transfer money, pay bills, set up standing orders and much more from the convenience of your own home.

- Electronic tills which read bar codes, thus reducing the time it takes to add up your shopping bill.

- Shopping online.

Activity 10.4: E-tailing versus retailing

From your own knowledge and experience, prepare some brief notes comparing the potential benefits and disadvantages of e-tailing and retailing for consumers.

Case Study – Centrica

This Case Study follows on from Session 3.

At Centrica, Simon Waugh, Director of Marketing and Managing Director of Financial Services dreams of being able to marry huge scale with fine detail by taking all the knowledge in the company's massive database and customising the service for every individual customer. "The key for me is to figure out how we bring back a high level of customer service, almost like a corner shop which knows you and all your needs, backed up by the strength, skills, scale and volume of a major player. That's the challenge: when you have millions of customers, how can you really look them in the eyes and say we can deal with you as a person; you aren't just a reference number?"

It's not just ambitious. It also needs investment – and lots of it, in people, technology and training. The difficulty for Waugh is making the business case for something that is going to pay off in the longer term but which will gobble up money in the short term. So for the last year he has been overseeing the trial of a new customer service 'laboratory' based in Leeds with 45 staff and 350,000 customers, to test the commercial value of different approaches to service delivery in terms of customer satisfaction, productivity, costs and income.

The customers of the lab are a cross-section of the database as a whole and represent different segments. Where the corner shop approach comes in is that customers speak with one person about all their products, whether British Gas, Goldfish or the Automobile Association, similar to key account management that suppliers use with their business customers. And because there are only 12 agents per team leader, rather than 20 as in all other call centres, the leader spends less time on administration and more on coaching, counselling and acting as mentor for individual staff.

Source: *Marketing Business*, September 2000.

Questions

1. How important do you think the P for People is for Centrica – what evidence can you read in the Case Study?

2. How is Centrica preparing its people to provide high standards of service?

3. What does the Case Study suggest are the difficulties for Centrica in the short term?

SUMMARY OF KEY POINTS

- Services have different characteristics to products that have implications for marketing.

- Services cannot be stored – they are consumed at the point of delivery. This has implications for the way organisations market and provide services.

- Services will always be inconsistent because of the human factor introducing variation each time the service is performed.

- The extended mix is used for marketing services – people, process and physical evidence.

- In many cases the person is the service, which has significant implications for advertising and promotion – it is their knowledge, skills, qualifications and experience that enable then to produce the service.

- By innovating processes, organisations may be able to gain competitive advantage through being able to offer a faster or more efficient or reliable service.

- The physical evidence includes the environment in which the service is delivered and paperwork that accompanies the service.

Improving and developing own learning

The following projects are designed to help you to develop your knowledge and skills further by carrying out some research yourself. Feedback is not provided for this type of learning because there are no 'answers' to be found, but you may wish to discuss your findings with colleagues and fellow students.

Project A

What services do you regularly use?

How effectively are they marketed?

What improvements can you suggest?

Project B

As above, consider the services that you use on a regular basis.

What is the significance of each of the 3Ps for each one?

Is one element more important than another in the efficient and effective delivery of that service?

Project C

What examples can you think of where ICT has significantly improved a service?

What were the main benefits?

Are there any disadvantages?

Feedback on activities

Activity 10.1: Fast food fact finding

Although there are no specific answers to this activity you probably found that you compared different aspects of the service such as:

- Speed.
- Reliability.
- Friendly, helpful staff.
- Cleanliness of premises.

You will all have had different experiences and have different opinions on what was good and what was bad. Tolerance of mistakes – wrong change given for example – will depend on the individual and what else happened – possibly how it was dealt with by the staff member concerned.

What you should have found is that although the product was the same – or almost the same – each time, the service was not. This makes the marketing of services more complex than the marketing of products.

Activity 10.2: Press release

NB: Press releases should be double spaced.

Logo.
News from Macey Communications plc.
Macey Communications plc.

5th October 200X

Celebrity chef, Paul Macey opens restaurant at Melton Manor, Melton, Cambs – October 200X

Melton Manor has been completely refurbished to create a homely and welcoming restaurant by celebrity chef, Paul Macey. The sixteenth-century manor house has been sympathetically modernised so many original features have been kept, such as the minstrel's gallery in the main dining area which used to be the banqueting hall. The colours throughout are rich and sumptuous with tapestries and wall hangings featuring in almost every room.

The restaurant opens on 25th October with a charity event for 100 invited guests and to the public on the following day. Food will be traditional with as many ingredients as possible sourced from local suppliers. Paul is keen to celebrate everything that is good about British food but also to bring in new ideas from all around the world.

He says, "We are aiming to create an exciting experience for our guests through the use of different combinations of foods on the menu from traditional roasts including goose and venison to Caribbean and Jamaican cuisine. As well as enjoying their meal in the restaurant, guests will be able to wander through our lovely gardens and perhaps listen to musicians in the rose garden and watch a play on the terraces. We have lots of ideas so will be ringing the changes throughout the seasons."

Ends

Notes to editors

Paul Macey has hosted the Good British Food programme on Universal TV for five years and has published several books featuring British dishes through the ages. He trained with the famous Wright brothers in the well-known London hotel

Burridges and in France and Italy working with Michel-jean and Ricardo Pavarotti respectively.

Further information from Gordon Pool, PR Manager, Macey Communications plc. Tel: 0207 123654. Email: gpool@macey.co.uk.

Page 1 of 1.

Macey Communications plc, 34 Polson Street, London SW6, Tel: 0207 123654, Fax: 0207 333555.

Activity 10.3: Misleading claims

Internal Memorandum

To: G. Patel
                HR Manager

From: D. Jones
                Marketing Manager

Date: 4th September 2002

Subject: Complaints about current recruitment advertising campaign

As you know, this campaign was launched a week before the recent industrial action significantly disrupted our operating schedules. The result of this has been passengers left stranded or let down, which has attracted a lot of local media coverage on television, radio and newspapers.

Although the campaign has been successful in attracting a record number of new applicants I am recommending that it be cancelled immediately. The reason is that we have now received, via the customer care department, three complaints that the advertisement is misleading. I suggest that we focus on other benefits rather than efficient service until we can prove that this is once more the case. I also make this recommendation following advice from the Advertising Standards Agency.

Activity 10.4: E-tailing versus retailing

The potential benefits and disadvantages of e-tailing and retailing for consumers could be presented in a table similar to the one set out below:

	Advantages	Disadvantages
E-tailing.	■ Convenience of home shopping. ■ Open 24/7. ■ Instant access to a wide range of products. ■ Easy ordering and payment. ■ One location!	■ Lack of personal interaction. ■ Home delivery problems. ■ Cannot examine goods.
Retailing.	■ Access to salespeople for information. ■ Opportunity to examine products. ■ Personal after-sales service.	■ Restricted opening hours. ■ Time consuming. ■ Travel costs. ■ Multiple sites.

Session 11

Planning the marketing budget

Introduction

Budgets are set to provide estimates for marketing and other forms of organisations' spending and guidelines for decision making. It is important that these are as accurate as possible because significant overspend in one area may mean that other important projects are delayed or cancelled.

This Session will raise awareness of how budgets are set and costs estimated and provide information on how to avoid overspend. It pulls together the references made to budget implications and cost allocation made in previous Sessions. You will find it useful to refer back to Session 6 which considered budget implications when organising marketing activities.

LEARNING OUTCOMES

At the end of this Session you will be able to:

- Demonstrate an ability to manipulate numbers in a marketing context.

- Explain the process used for setting a budget and apportioning fixed and overhead costs.

- Make recommendations on alternative courses of action.

Marketing budgets

Budget implications and cost have been referred to throughout this Companion because every activity has a cost. The cost is offset against the income generated so marketers can make informed decisions in the future about the cost effectiveness of how things have been done in the past.

The overall marketing budget will cover different areas of activity so there will be an event budget, PR budget, advertising budget, sponsorship budget etc. Different marketing activities will generally be allocated different amounts according to the size of the contribution it is expected to make towards achievement of the marketing objectives. Therefore if a major new sponsorship deal is planned to raise brand awareness, then a higher percentage of the marketing budget may be allocated to the sponsorship budget that year.

The Marketing Manager, or person responsible for budget administration, will check actual against estimated spending as the budget for each area is allocated to different activities during the year. Overspending in one area may mean that later activities have to be reduced, so any significant variance (between actual and estimated) has to be accounted for. Throughout this Companion, budget implications have been referred to and Session 5 on planning considered how costs should be estimated and allocated when planning activities so expenses can be controlled when the plan is implemented. The more accurately this is done, the easier it is to monitor and the more likely that overspend will be avoided.

A budget is a financial plan for a period that sets out the revenues and costs involved. If the marketer can estimate the benefits – financial and otherwise – that a particular investment will bring then he/she can assess the feasibility of going ahead with that plan. Part of the planning process also involves evaluating risks. These are not always financial but most have an additional cost involved. For example, failure to realise that the competition is launching a high profile advertising campaign at the same time as yours may mean that additional, unplanned activities need to be introduced to give further support to your brand.

Any activity that is planned takes place in the future and therefore it is possible that hidden costs may emerge or the situation change, so that the plan is not implemented as expected. Following an activity, marketers should evaluate the plan and determine whether it should be repeated or not. Part of the evaluation process should investigate whether increased costs – if they occurred – could have been prevented or whether the activity was not as viable as initial calculations identified. Reviewing different activities and evaluating effectiveness is discussed in the next and final Session.

Activity 11.1: Trading down!

Mop and Brush Monthly is a trade magazine sold directly to cleaning agencies via annual subscription by MB Publishing. The Marketing Manager is reviewing figures for last year (shown below). Subscription costs were not increased the previous year and stand at £60 for 10 issues a year. Advertising costs are £2,500 for a full page (full colour) for products and services and £1,500 for recruitment. Advertising sales were disappointing last year despite the increase in subscriptions.

	Predicted sales 2001/02	Budgeted sales £ 2001/02	Actual sales 2001/02	Actual sales £ 2001/02
Subscription sales(renewals)	1,500	90,000	1,633	97,980
Subscription sales(new)	100	6,000	246	14,760
Advertising sales (products and services)	100	250,000	83	207,500
Advertising sales (recruitment)	125 pages	187,500	86	129,000
TOTAL SALES REVENUE		447,100		347,774
Printing and distribution costs		120,000		127,000
Salaries		80,000		62,000
Direct marketing costs		15,000		11,250
Advertising costs		4,000		4,000
Miscellaneous		13,000		13,000
TOTAL COSTS		232,000		217,250
CONTRIBUTION		215,100		130,524

Answer the following questions:

1.   What reasons can you suggest for the disappointing advertising sales?

2.   What suggestions can you make to improve sales next year?

Compare your ideas to those of fellow students to see how many different ideas you can come up with for improving sales next year.

Collecting information for budget setting

It can be appreciated that before a budget can be developed, data and information needs to be gathered from different sources.

Internal sources include:

- Project evaluation reports.

- Key personnel – for example, if setting the events budget, the marketer might discuss the cost of previous activities and the merits of different suppliers to determine whether cost savings are possible or if they gave value for money, etc.

- Internal documentation on money spent on related activities in the recent past.

External sources include:

- Current suppliers.

- Potential suppliers.

- Competitor spending.

When planning activities it is rare that cost is not a constraint for marketers so it is important to set budgets so that money available can be used effectively, and spread over the activities that need to happen in order to achieve objectives. Activities may need to be prioritised if the budget for the current year is less than the previous one and similar activities are planned. Justifying costs and budget decisions are explored in the final Session.

Methods used to set budgets

Different methods or approaches are used to set budgets. For completely new ventures, such as the early dotcoms, where there is little previous information and investment in lots of activities is required, the approach might be to look at what competitors will be spending and try to do more. In this case, marketing oriented organisations might consider spending as much as possible to make an impression and review the cost effectiveness of each activity before setting the budget for the next year. The question they cannot answer in advance – because there is no information available on market structure, buyer behaviour etc. – is what the result will be. Calculating how much revenue will be achieved by spending money on certain activities is key for marketers setting budgets. If this is known then costs can be allocated to the activities that will bring in the most revenue.

Some of the common methods of setting budgets are described below:

- Historically-based budgets – the previous year's budget is adjusted for inflation and any other known cost increases from suppliers etc. This is a fairly simple exercise but is unlikely to be effective because it fails to consider properly what needs to be done in the future, which may be very different from what was done in the past. Sometimes this is known as SALT – Same As Last Time and may not carry an adjustment for inflation.

- Percentage of sales – this may be based on historical figures or future projections of sales. If sales are expected to fall, the marketing budget might be adjusted downwards from the previous year so the money has to be more wisely spent to achieve the same level of communication with stakeholders. Alternatively, justification for increasing the percentage figure may be made for new products to increase growth and market share.

- By task or objective – a more complex exercise that explores what marketing objectives and tasks need to be done for the year and what each is likely to cost. These may range from product launches, exhibitions, increasing advertising, decreasing sales promotions etc. This approach is based on needs.

Activity 11.2: Budget setting

Last year, ABC Training exhibited at the National Training Exhibition and has decided to do so again. The budget for last year's show was £50,000 which was exceeded by £10,000 due to an unplanned cost of replacing the organisation's exhibition stand. Major costs incurred last year were £10,000 for salaries, £10,000 for exhibition space and £30,000 for other costs. No increase in costs is expected this year apart from a 2.5% increase in salary costs. The sales directly attributed to this event were £580,000.

What budget would you recommend if using:

i) SALT method?

ii) Percentage of sales method?

iii) Task/cost method?

Activity 11.3: Memo to manager

For the above event, write a memo to the marketing manager recommending the budget for next year's exhibition.

Justify your decision.

What will it cost?

Whether setting a budget for a single activity such as a corporate hospitality event or the advertising budget for the year, it is necessary to estimate what the costs are and how much each will be. When costing a project always add contingency – an additional sum because some costs will be more than expected. This may be because a supplier puts charges up or hidden costs emerge.

Costs can be divided into direct costs that relate to those that form part of the finished item and indirect costs (overheads) which are related to the organisation as a whole, or the process. The direct costs of producing a brochure are labour costs (designers, copy editors, photographer, printer etc.) and materials (paper, ink, special print effects etc.) whereas the indirect costs are related to the use of premises and machinery.

Fixed and variable costs

Costs may also be classified as fixed, variable and stepped according to how they behave!

- Fixed costs are not dependent on the level of activity. Thus for a factory they are rent, rates, heating and lighting because they remain static no matter whether one production line is running or several.

- Variable costs vary according to the level of activity. For example, the greater quantity of product that is being produced, the greater the amount of raw materials used; so costs go up in line with activity and vice versa.

  Some costs have a fixed and a variable part. Telephone costs have a fixed rental charge but the cost of the calls made increases with the number of telephone calls made.

- Stepped costs rise at certain points according to the level of activity. For example, if one production line made 200 units per week there would be a certain level of variable cost. If it had to work to full capacity to make 250 units per week then costs would increase due to the additional costs of extra labour and raw materials. However, if the factory was required to produce 300 units per week, due to a new order from sales, then they would have to build an additional production line. Costs would rise significantly (or be stepped up) if the factory produced more than 250 units per week. If each production line had a capacity of 250 then the next step would be at 501 units per week.

Another point to consider is the revenue from the extra 50 units per week. If this does not cover the cost of the new line it might not be cost effective to take the order for the additional 50 units per week. This is an illustration of how closely the different functions of an organisation need to work together. Action by one impacts on another. If Production could cover the cost of a new line by making an additional 100 units then they might encourage Sales to find additional customers or sell more to existing customers in order to take the new order.

Activity 11.4: Break-even

Break-even point is the point at which organisations begin to make a profit, when the revenue from sales is greater than the total of the fixed and variable costs. It is one of the ways in which organisations assess the viability of opportunities, marketing initiatives and projects. The aim is to find the point at which the income or profits cover the outlay. Organisations also use a number of more sophisticated techniques for this, which you will cover at later stages of your studies.

The formula for calculating break-even is:

$$\text{Break-even point} = \frac{\text{Fixed costs}}{(\text{Selling price} - \text{Variable costs per unit})}$$

A toy manufacturer is planning to introduce a new car. Calculate the point at which break-even on the production costs occurs using the following information:

Selling price of toy car   £10.00.
Variable cost   £5.00 per unit.
Fixed costs   £100,000.

Look at Dibb, Simkin, Pride & Ferrell, *Marketing Concepts and Strategies*, Houghton Mifflin 2001, Chapter 19, pp. 597-598 to see how this might be represented as a graph.

Apportioning marketing costs

As previously mentioned, organisations incur direct and indirect costs. When presenting the budget the marketer will need to identify how marketing costs can be apportioned. This is sometimes referred to as splitting the costs. There are several approaches to this:

- **Time-based costing**

  If carrying out a project for a business unit then marketing can estimate the number of man hours required and charge an agreed amount per hour.

- **Apportioning costs by ratio**

  Organisations often spread marketing costs across their different business units according to ratio of turnover or sales. Thus the unit with the lowest sales will be charged the least amount and the one with the highest sales the most, as it is assumed that use of the service is split accordingly.

- **Apportioning advertising costs by space/time**

  A useful way of apportioning advertising costs. If the advertisement features one product then all costs will be apportioned to that product. If two products are featured then the advertising costs are shared equally. However, if one product is featured more heavily than the other then the costs may be shared unequally, so the product that receiving the greatest exposure bears the greater cost.

- **Activity-based costing**

  Sharing costs this way is probably the most accurate but is not always easy. Each activity or task is identified and its cost estimated or measured according to how long it takes and how much that time costs. For example, the cost of producing a quarterly in-house newsletter might be calculated as follows:

Time spent per year	200 hours
No. of newsletters per year	4
Cost per hour	£20
Cost of producing single newsletter	50 x £20 = £1,000

Activity 11.5: Cutting costs

In the example above it is calculated that the cost of producing a company newsletter is £1,000. Imagine that you are responsible for producing that newsletter four times a year but have been told that due to a cost cutting exercise you will only be able to produce three a year.

Why might activity-based costing be significant and useful in this situation?

Considering different options

There are often situations when it becomes obvious that the estimated cost of the activities planned is too high. The marketer must consider alternative course of action such as:

- Identifying activities that can be postponed until more money becomes available.

- Prioritising activities and allocating spending to them first.

- Negotiating better discounts with suppliers.

- Using less expensive suppliers.

- Sharing costs with others – collaborative advertising, promotions.

Cutting costs is very important in today's competitive environment so marketers must continually be looking for ways of being more cost effective. However, they must also look for additional ways of increasing revenue by measuring cost effectiveness more exactly so that they plan more of the activities that bring in the best results. Supermarkets in the UK have found that it is not sufficient to 'squeeze' suppliers continually by negotiating lower and lower payments. Ethically, consumers expect organisations to behave responsibly towards suppliers.

Activity 11.6: Options, options!

It is often very difficult to make decisions about different options because you are not always comparing like with like. Visit www.english-heritage.org.uk and click on Heritage Hospitality for an example of this.

You will notice that there different costs and specifications for each of the venues, so that if you were trying to make a decision on where to hold a dinner based on cost, it would prove a very difficult choice.

Considering what you have studied so far in this Companion, can you suggest some way of simplifying the decision making process so that you are comparing like with like?

Case Study – The Christmas catalogue: Wallbury's Plc

Wallbury's is a well-established retailer with 29 stores throughout the country and a turnover in excess of £300 million. It has a successful retail formula selling a broad range of products in six categories:

- Toys.
- Books.
- Clothing.
- Cosmetics.
- CDs/Videos.
- Electrical goods.

Each of the above categories is managed by a team comprising a product manager, group buyer, merchandiser and either one or two assistants.

The marketing department produces an annual catalogue for the group that is distributed in early October. Individual product groups also hold budgets and brief their own advertising agencies in collaboration with the marketing department.

Like many retailers, Wallbury's sales build to a peak in December and success in this period is crucial. Wallbury's marketing activity reflects this peak and a major component of its seasonal push is the Christmas catalogue. Work starts on producing this in January, several months before it is distributed. Indeed, visuals and layouts are usually ready by June for the October launch. All staff working on the catalogue know that it is critical that it is launched in October, as 30% of annual sales are taken during November and December. Therefore final deadlines for amendments are late September to allow a month for printing and distribution.

Comprising 32 pages, typesetting and preparation cost £100,000 and take 2 weeks with a further week needed for checking proofs. Print costs amount to £50 per thousand copies. Each page needs an average of six photographs and these cost £50 each including photography.

Some of the costs of producing the catalogues can be recovered from the manufacturers of the good featured in its pages. It has become established practice to sell the prime advertising space on the front cover for £10,000, the back cover for £5,000, with the remaining pages being sold for an average of £2,000 each.

Half the photographs are available from the suppliers, so saving some costs. A complex part of managing the entire project is negotiating with suppliers about which products are to be included in the catalogue. This takes up to three months and it is during this time that the marketing department negotiates with suppliers about advertising in the catalogue. In recent years it has been more and more difficult to sell the space on the inside pages as suppliers find it difficult to measure the return on their investment.

Source: CIM Marketing in Practice examination paper, December 2000.

Questions

1. Draw up an estimate of the costs associated with producing a million copies of the catalogue, together with likely suppliers' contributions.

2. If it appears likely that the revenue for advertising sales on inside pages will be significantly reduced, what suggestions can you make for reducing costs?

3. Wallbury's is considering producing a full online catalogue, prior to selling selected products online. What might their first actions be before setting a budget for this?

> **SUMMARY OF KEY POINTS**
>
> - A budget is an estimate of planned expenditure and should be as accurate as possible.
>
> - When setting budgets there are a number of methods that can be used including historical, percentage of sales and activity/cost method.
>
> - When estimating costs, marketers should review previous expenditure and look for cost savings such as negotiating discounts from suppliers and reducing the number of activities undertaken.
>
> - Add a contingency to the budget figure to cover unexpected expenditure.
>
> - The cost of marketing services should be spread across all activities and there are various ways of apportioning or splitting these costs – according to the nature of the activity.
>
> - Techniques such as break-even analysis are used to assess the viability of, and make decisions about, competing options.

Improving and developing own learning

The following projects are designed to help you to develop your knowledge and skills further by carrying out some research yourself. Feedback is not provided for this type of learning because there are no 'answers' to be found but you may wish to discuss your findings with colleagues and fellow students.

> **Project A**
>
> Imagine that you have invented a new product and wish to obtain money from backers or sponsors to plan for a spectacular launch.
>
> Identify what activities you need to undertake and how much they will cost.
>
> How can you justify the sum you require for your budget?

Project B

Think of a marketing event that you would like to host.

Imagine that you are planning to take a series of half-page advertisements in a local newspaper to advertise the event and have a budget for four insertions.

What budget would you need? (Check the rate card of your local newspaper).

What results do you expect?

What else could you do to advertise the event?

What would that cost?

If there was no additional budget available how would you reduce the advertising to pay for other activities?

Project C

Consider the last holiday or event that you planned. What did it cost?

What cost savings did you make when planning?

Why were you able to achieve these?

Then review the main suppliers that you currently use within your organisation.

Do they give customer satisfaction?

How much do their products and services cost in relation to competitors?

If they are more expensive than other suppliers that you might use, what added value are you paying for?

If you are not able to do this in your job role consider a supplier you use at home – for example, utility services.

Feedback on activities

Activity 11.1: Trading down!

1. The salary costs were lower than budget, suggesting that there was a staff shortage, thus reducing the ability of the organisation to operate at full capacity. This may mean that key advertising accounts were not serviced properly. This supports the fact that direct marketing costs were lower so reduced activity here might be a significant factor in not attracting companies to advertise their products and services. This might also have a knock-on effect on recruitment advertising.

2. Recruiting additional staff or using agency staff to ensure full productivity would help. However, there are other ways to stimulate advertising through keeping in touch with key accounts and offering special deals for increasing advertising. As subscriptions are higher than expected, the magazine is popular and the price could be increased. It may be necessary to increase advertising rates but this must be considered against the need to increase the volume. There might be opportunities to promote the magazine via trade shows and exhibitions.

3. The publishers may also consider an online version of their magazine and increase advertising revenue by encouraging companies to use banner advertisements linked to editorial. These can be charged at a much higher rate than standard banner advertising.

Activity 11.2: Budget setting

1. Same as last time would probably mean that a budget of £50,000 would be allocated and the additional 2.5% increase on salary costs absorbed. This would be reasonable as the budget was sufficient last year except for the cost of the stand, the cost of which would not be incurred again. The organisation might also review last year's figures to see if any cost savings were possible to help absorb the additional salary costs.

2. Percentage of sales is usually between 5 and 15 per cent. Taking a 10 per cent figure would give a budget of £58,000, which would allow the organisation to look at ways of improving last year's exhibition presentation or consider additional publicity to raise greater awareness of company products and services.

3.   The cost of two tasks associated with the exhibition are identified – £10,000 for space and £10,250 for staff. To calculate the other costs it would be necessary to look at last year's figures, identify tasks and costs and review if these would be take place again, and at what cost. Finally, any new tasks should also be costed and added to the budget.

Activity 11.3: Memo to manager

ABC Training
Internal Memorandum

To: Chris Fenton
                 Marketing Manager

From: Elisha Herr
                 Events Executive

Date: 7th September 2002

Subject: National Training Show, 12th-17th July 2003

Following our recent meeting, I have reviewed last year's figures and recommend that a budget of £65,000 be made available for the planning and organising of the exhibition stand at the above show.

Major costs are similar to last year as shown below:

Space	10,000
Staff	10,250
Printed materials	15,000
Planning costs	5,000
Publicity	10,000
Equipment hire	5,000
Total	55,250

However, there a new product will be launched at next year's show so additional publicity and activities will need to be planned. An additional £10,000 would be required for the options that are currently being considered and in the light of the excellent sales results from last year I recommend that these go ahead.

I will contact you next week to discuss the figures further and have put it on the agenda for our next events planning meeting on 4th November.

Activity 11.4: Break-even

Break-even point   = 100,000/(10-5).

                               = 100,000/5.

                               = 20,000 units.

Therefore, the company makes a profit once they produce more than 20,000 units. Break-even occurs at cash sales of £200,000 (20,000 x £10 selling price per unit).

Activity 11.5: Cutting costs

It is useful to be able to identify costs for specific activities if these need to be reduced to cut costs. In this example, if it is decided to produce only three newsletters per year then £3,000 will be put into the budget for this instead of £4,000. However, it may be that one issue always takes more time because it is a 'bigger issue' so an additional figure for contingency may need to be added on or this larger issue may not be feasible unless costs can be reduced elsewhere to allow for this.

Activity 11.6: Options!

One of the easiest ways to do this is to add up all the costs associated with holding the event at the venue and then divide the total by the number of people attending. This will give you a cost per head and can be done for each venue so you will be comparing like with like in terms of cost.

Session 12

Presenting and evaluating the marketing budget

Introduction

Marketers need to be able to use financial data to help make decisions about future spending. This includes measuring the effectiveness of previous investments and budgets, and using new information to justify budgetary decisions for the future. In presenting a budget, marketers need to be able to argue its feasibility and explain how budgets have been constructed and what controls have been factored in. This Session will help marketers contribute effectively to this process and follows on from the previous one which discussed budget setting and initial preparation.

LEARNING OUTCOMES

At the end of this Session you will be able to:

- Explain how organisations assess the viability of opportunities, marketing initiatives and projects.

- Prepare, present and justify a budget as the basis for decision making on marketing promotion.

- Examine the correlation between marketing mix decisions and results.

- Evaluate the cost effectiveness of a marketing budget, including a review of suppliers and activities.

Evaluating cost effectiveness across the marketing mix

When studying the planning and organising of marketing events you considered the cost effectiveness of different activities. In simple terms this is an attempt to measure whether money was well spent on this activity to make it easier to decide whether it is worth doing again.

The marketing budget covers all activities carried out by the marketing function in order to achieve their objectives. The marketing mix elements are interrelated as discussed in Sessions 8, 9 and 10. It is often difficult to measure exactly the contribution that each made at any one time because activities are planned to support each other so the final result is greater that that which would have been

217

achieved if each went on independently. However, when planning how to allocate the budget across the different activities it is necessary to review the revenue achieved by each to determine, for example, if the current sponsorship deal be extended or less advertising is required this year for certain product lines.

You will also appreciate that product, price, promotion and place decisions depend on a number of other factors including new opportunities, emerging threats and competitor activity. New opportunities might be new channels of distribution such as online retailing so a greater portion of the budget is allocated to this element of the mix than the previous year. When presenting the budget, the marketer needs to be able to justify why money is being spent as set out, so understanding what needs to be achieved and why is critical to the arguments and reasons that need to be put forward.

Activity 12.1: Eye opener!

As the Marketing Manager of a medium-sized retail opticians, you are planning the opening of a new outlet in a busy shopping centre. Your budget is £10,000. The options you are considering are:

Advertising in local newspapers including production	£3,000 per half page.
Celebrity (local football player)	£5,000.
Local radio advertising	£200 per 2 minute slot.
Cost of radio advertising production	£1,500.
Giveaways – baseball caps with logo	£1,000 for 500.

The shopping centre is in a large market town which has a very successful football club with a number of popular national team players. The local population are mainly families (ACORN classification mainly CDs). Prepare some notes to help you present your decision on what marketing support you are recommending for this opening. You have very good relationships with local media and have been able to negotiate up to a 10% discount on broadcast and print advertising in the past.

Reviewing expenditure

The marketer should constantly be monitoring costs and reviewing expenditure. Monitoring is a constant process, whereas review is a periodic check to identify what happened against what was planned.

When evaluating what happened to expenditure a simple checklist can speed up the process:

- What was the budget set?
- Were all activities achieved as planned?
- What were the variances? How accurate were original costings?
- What cost more?
- What cost less?
- Where could cost savings have been made?
- What caused the variances? What control did we have over the causes?
- What lessons have been learnt?

This provides information for future planners but also for budget holders. For example, if a new supplier had been used and was able to provide services at lower rate than existing suppliers then the marketer may consider using the new supplier more often. Alternatively, he/she may use this information as a bargaining position and try to renegotiate terms with existing suppliers because they are more reliable.

Each activity provides more information about cost and effectiveness for the marketer. This needs to be considered against the objectives of the next activity. The decision made must be in-line with objectives and priorities. A more expensive supplier may be used because reliability is more important than cost.

Presenting the budget

There are a number of key questions that marketers need to be prepared for when presenting a budget:

- What will it cost? (What do we have to pay?)
- How are costs to be apportioned? (Who is going to pay for it?)
- What will the result be?
- Why is it worth doing?

In addition, the marketer needs to be able to articulate:

- The budget objectives.
- The activities planned to achieve the objectives.
- Justification for decisions taken.

As previously mentioned, preparing detailed costings so estimates are as accurate as possible, is essential. When presenting, make good use of graphs and charts to show anticipated costs, expected revenue and how costs will be apportioned.

Justification for decisions made may be purely financial but will also be related to other factors. For example, increased competitor advertising or the need to increase sales temporarily, so an additional direct mailing is planned because it has previously achieved excellent results in this area. The cost of that additional activity then needs to be justified. Influencing effectively demands that the marketer presents the whole picture, giving reasoned arguments for planned activities and justifying the costs involved.

When presenting the cost benefit of planned activities, remember that these will not always be purely financial and may be spread over a considerable period of time. The benefits of PR activities and sponsorship are difficult to measure in quantitative terms – look back at Session 8. Training staff in customer care skills should increase customer service and satisfaction levels, but the return on this investment is difficult to measure because it is long term and difficult to isolate. In this case the marketer might present this as a way of contributing towards the company objective of reducing customer complaints. The cost of the training can then be offset against the money saved by reducing the number of complaints dealt with.

Activity 12.2: Presenting the budget

As a Marketing Assistant in a financial services company, you are presenting the budget you have prepared for a corporate hospitality event. You are hosting a lunch at a polo game for 100 clients. The food and drink is costing £25 per head and you have decided to provide a small gift of a pen for each guest. You have assembled the guest list after consulting the four key account managers and are confident that the list contains your most profitable and loyal clients. However, you would like to include some 20 new clients but this will mean that you need to hire a larger marquee and four additional hospitality staff. This will take you over your budget of £8,000.

What do you decide to do?

The marquee for 100 guests plus 15 staff from the host company costs £2,000 and the next size up costs £3,000.

Prepare some slides for the final presentation.

Case Study – Property exhibitions

Memorandum

To: Marketing, Tattersfield Property Holdings plc

From: G. van der Bilt, Project Management

Subject: Property Exhibitions, Tattersfield Property Holdings plc

I would very much appreciate the marketing department's assistance in arranging stands and organising the staffing at the following two exhibitions.

Europrop 200X Berlin

This is the three-day show we attended last year, which generated the lead that led to the sale of 50,000 metres of factory space. Stand costs are likely to be higher this year, but the organisers are promising an increase in attendance of 25%. Other costs are around the same. I have looked at last year's costs for a 50-metre stand and they are:

Stand space (per day)	£6,000
Stand design	£6,000
Staffing	£200 per day (4 staff)
Travel	£200 each
Hotels, food, expenses	£2,700

Chicago industrial real estate fair

This is a new event, and the organisers expect a quality attendance of around 1,000 leading industrialists. This takes place over four days, and a 40 square yard space costs $6,000 per day, with a 60 square yard space costing 50% more. Stand design costs are approximately half those of Europrop whilst other expenses are broadly similar except air fares and travel are likely to cost £300 per person. (NB: Assume $1.50 = £1.00)

I look forward to a successful attendance at both events as our research indicates that they offer excellent opportunities to reach key decision makers.

Source: CIM Marketing in Practice examination paper, December 1999.

Questions

1. Due to budget cutbacks it has been decided that the company can afford to attend only one of the two exhibitions mentioned in the memo. Identify costings for each event.

2. Make a recommendation for attending one of the events and justify.

3. What additional information would be useful to help make a final decision about which exhibition to attend?

SUMMARY OF KEY POINTS

- It is important to review actual against estimated spend to identify the reason for variances.

- When reviewing previous expenditure it is important to be able to identify where future cost savings can be made.

- When presenting the budget the marketer must be able to articulate what the money will be spent on, what the result will be and how costs will be covered.

- When justifying budget decisions, the marketer should be able to present a reasoned argument on what options have been considered and why the final decision was made.

Improving and developing own learning

The following projects are designed to help you to develop your knowledge and skills further by carrying out some research yourself. Feedback is not provided for this type of learning because there are no 'answers' to be found, but you may wish to discuss your findings with colleagues and fellow students.

Project A

Look at the current marketing budget for you organisation, or one you know well.

How has the money been allocated in relation to last year?

Are the same activities taking place or is there a different mix?

How might the differences be explained?

Project B

Review how marketing costs are apportioned in your organisation, or one you know well.

Which method or methods are used?

What improvements can you suggest?

How easy is it to identify how costs should be apportioned?

Project C

Try to arrange to sit in on a meeting when a budget is being presented.

Consider how well it was done. Were the decisions well made and justified?

How sure were the presenters of achieving results? Why?

If it was your money would you release it for this budget?

Now think of the last event you planned for yourself and friends or family or at work. How would you answer the question, 'Was it worth doing?'

Feedback on activities

Activity 12.1: Eye opener!

Situation

Opening of newest and largest retail outlet for EYE-2-EYE Opticians.

Aims and objectives

- To raise awareness of the new optical outlet among local population.

- To inform local population of services provided.

- To achieve widespread media coverage in both print and broadcast media immediately following the event, including photograph and editorial in the local paper and headline news on local radio.

Strategy

- Hire local celebrity to open outlet.

- Advertise local radio.

- Offer sales promotion for one month following launch.

Tactics

- Local radio advertising 2 weeks before launch.

- On the day, celebrity to cut tape to open and receive tour of premises including eye test and free pair of prescription spectacles (if required) and sunglasses.

- Invite local press – organise photo opportunities.

- Arrange for EYE-2-EYE Managing Director to be interviewed on local radio on the day of the launch.

- Give away baseball caps to public attending launch.

- Brief staff at outlet and marketing assistants who will be attending launch.

- News releases to local press.

- Poster in window of new outlet and other local branches.

- Sales promotion linked to newspaper advertisement – cut out coupon for 25% off new spectacles.

- Write up in in-house newsletter.

Budget (main activities)

Celebrity (local football player)	5,000
Local radio advertising (7 slots 10% discount)	1,260
Cost of radio advertising production	1,500
Baseball caps (500)	500
Press advertisement (10% discount on quarter page)	1,350
Posters	200
Total	£9,810

There is also a cost for the promotion but it is assumed that that will come from another budget.

Note the use of a structure SOST – Situation, Objectives, Strategy, Tactics. If resourcing the plan could use SOST + 6Ms or SOSTAC (Action & Control).

Activity 12.2: presenting the budget

There are no right or wrong answers. In this case the marketing assistant has decided to recommend that new clients be invited because it gives them an opportunity to meet satisfied customers and thus hear recommendations.

If there was no flexibility in the budget, then the recommendation might be to reduce the number of existing clients or to go with the original proposal. Note the presentation details what the objectives are, what it will cost and what the results should be. When presenting a budget a cost benefit analysis is a useful tool to use.

___

Objectives

- To reward loyal clients.
- To gather feedback from customers.
- To inform new clients of product range.
- To communicate image and brand.
- To introduce new clients to existing customers.

___

Budget

Food and drink (135 people)	3,375
Marquee	3,000
Gifts	1,000
Staff	500
Other	1,500
Total	£9,375

Results

- Reinforce brand and image.
- Feedback on company products and services.
- Face to face contact with customers.
- Sales leads (results from previous events).

Glossary

Glossary

Above-the-line – advertising for which a payment is made and for which a commission is paid to the advertising agency.

Account management – the process by which an agency or supplier manages the needs of a client.

ACORN (A Classification of Residential Neighbourhoods) – a database which divides up the entire population of the UK in terms of housing in which they live.

Added value – the increase in worth of a product or service as a result of a particular activity – in the context of marketing this might be packaging or branding.

Advertising – promotion of a product, service or message by an identified sponsor using paid-for media.

AIDA (Attention, Interest, Desire, Action) – a model describing the process that advertising or promotion is intended to initiate in the mind of a prospective customer.

Ansoff Matrix – model relating marketing strategy to general strategic direction. It maps product/market strategies.

BCG Matrix – model for product portfolio analysis.

Below-the-line – non-media advertising or promotion when no commission has been paid to the advertising agency.

Brand – the set of physical attributes of a product or service, together with the beliefs and expectations surrounding it.

Business plan – a strategic document showing cash flow, forecasts and direction of a company.

Business strategy – the means by which a business works towards achieving its stated aims.

Business to business (b2b) – relating to the sale of a product for any use other than personal consumption.

Business to consumer (b2c) – relating to the sale of a product for personal consumption.

Buying behaviour – the process that buyers go through when deciding whether or not to purchase goods or services.

Channels – the methods used by a company to communicate and interact with its customers.

Comparative advertising – advertising which compares a company's product with that of competing brands.

Competitive advantage – the product, proposition or benefit that puts a company ahead of its competitors.

Confusion marketing – controversial strategy of deliberately confusing the customer.

Consumer – individual who buys and uses a product or service.

Consumer behaviour – the buying habits and patterns of consumers in the acquisition and usage of products and services.

Copyright – the law that protects the originator's material from unauthorised use, usually (in the UK) for seventy years after the originator's death.

Corporate identity – the character a company seeks to establish for itself in the mind of the public.

Corporate reputation – a complex mix of characteristics such as ethos, identity and image that go to make up a company's public personality.

Culture – a shared set of values, beliefs and traditions that influence prevailing behaviour within a country or organisation.

Customer – a person or company who purchases goods or services.

Customer loyalty – feelings or attitudes that incline a customer to return to a company, shop or outlet to purchase there again.

Customer Relationship Management (CRM) – the coherent management of contacts and interactions with customers.

Customer satisfaction – the provision of goods or services which fulfil the customer's expectations in terms of quality and service, in relation to price paid.

DAGMAR (Defining Advertising Goals for Measured Advertising Response) – a model for planning advertising in such a way that its success can be quantitatively monitored.

Data processing – the obtaining, recording and holding of information which can then be retrieved, used, disseminated or erased.

Data Protection Act – a law which makes organisations responsible for protecting the privacy of personal data.

Database marketing – whereby customer information stored in an electronic database is utilised for targeting marketing activities.

Decision Making Unit (DMU) – the team of people in an organisation or family group who make the final buying decision.

Demographic data – information describing and segmenting a population in terms of age, sex, income and so on which can be used to target marketing campaigns.

Differentiation – ensuring that products and services have a unique element to allow them to stand out from the rest.

Direct mail – delivery of an advertising or promotional message to customers or potential customers by mail.

Direct marketing – all activities that make it possible to offer goods or services or to transmit other messages to a segment of the population by post, telephone, email or other direct means.

Direct Response Advertising – advertising incorporating a contact method such as a phone number or enquiry form with the intention of encouraging the recipient to respond directly to the advertiser.

Distribution (Place) – the process of getting the goods from the manufacturer or supplier to the user.

Diversification – an increase in the variety of goods and services produced by an organisation.

E-commerce – business conducted electronically.

E-marketing – marketing conducted electronically.

Electronic Point of Sale (EPOS) – a system whereby electronic tills are used to process customer transactions in a retail outlet.

Ethical marketing – marketing that takes account of the moral aspects of decisions.

Export marketing – the marketing of goods or services to overseas customers.

Field marketing – extending an organisation's marketing in the field through merchandising, product launches, training of retail staff, etc.

FMCG (Fast Moving Consumer Goods) – such as packages of food and toiletries.

Focus groups – a tool for marketing research where small groups of participants take part in guided discussions on the topic being researched.

Forecasting – calculation of future events and performance.

Franchising – the selling of a licence by the owner (franchisor) to a third party (franchisee) permitting the sale of a product or service for a specified period.

Geo-demographics – a method of analysis combining geographic and demographic variables.

Grey market (silver market) – term used to define a population over a certain age (usually 65).

Industrial marketing (or business to business marketing) – the marketing of industrial products.

Innovation – development of new products, services or ways of working.

Internal customers – employees within an organisation viewed as 'consumers' of a product or service provided by another part of the organisation.

Internal marketing – the process of eliciting support for a company and its activities among its own employees in order to encourage them to promote its goals.

International marketing – the conduct and co-ordination of marketing activities in more than one country.

Key account management – account management as applied to a company's most valuable customers.

Logo – a graphic usually consisting of a symbol and or group of letters that identifies a company or brand.

Macro environment – the external factors which affect companies' planning and performance, and are beyond its control. (SLEPT).

Market development – the process of growing sales by offering existing products (or new versions of them) to new customer groups.

Market penetration – the attempt to grow one's business by obtaining a larger market share in an existing market.

Market research – the gathering and analysis of data relating to markets to inform decision making.

Marketing research – the gathering and analysis of data relating to marketing to inform decision making (includes product research, place research, pricing research, etc.).

Market segmentation – the division of the marketplace into distinct sub-groups or segments, each characterised by particular tastes and requiring a specific marketing mix.

Market share – a company's sales of a given product or set of products to a given set of customers expressed as a percentage of total sales of all such products to such customers.

Marketing audit – scrutiny of an organisation's existing marketing system to ascertain its strengths and weaknesses.

Marketing communications (Promotion) – all methods used by a firm to communicate with its customers and stakeholders.

Marketing information – any information used or required to support marketing decisions.

Marketing mix – the combination of marketing inputs that affect customer motivation and behaviour (7 Ps – Product, Price, Promotion, Place, People, Process and Physical Evidence).

Marketing orientation – a business strategy whereby customers' needs and wants determine corporate direction.

Marketing planning – the selection and scheduling of activities to support the company's chosen marketing strategy or goals.

Marketing strategy – the broad methods chosen to achieve marketing objectives.

Micro environment – the immediate context of a company's operations, including such elements as suppliers, customers and competitors.

Mission statement – a company's summary of business philosophy, purpose and direction.

Model – simplified representation of a process, designed to aid in understanding.

New Product Development (NPD) – the creation of new products from evaluation of proposals through to launch.

Niche marketing – the marketing of a product to a small and well-defined segment of the marketplace.

Objectives – a company's defined and measurable aims or goals for a given period.

Packaging – material used to protect and promote goods.

Personal selling – one-to-one communication between seller and prospective purchaser.

PIMS (Profit Impact of Marketing Strategies) – a US database supplying data such as environment, strategy, competition and internal data.

Porter's Five Forces – an analytic model developed by Michael E. Porter which analyses the competitive environment and industry structure.

Positioning – the creation of an image for a product or service in the minds of customers, both specifically to that item and in relation to competitive offerings.

Product life cycle – a model describing the progress of a product from the inception of the idea through the peak of sales, to its decline.

Promotional mix – the components of an individual campaign which are likely to include advertising, personal selling, public relations, direct marketing, packaging and sales promotion.

Public Relations (PR) – the planned and sustained communication to promote mutual understanding between an organisation and its stakeholders.

Pull promotion – addresses the customer directly with a view to getting them to demand the product and hence 'pull' it down through the distribution chain.

Push promotion – relies on the next link in the distribution chain, e.g. wholesaler, to 'push' out products to the customer.

Qualitative research – information that cannot be measured or expressed in numeric terms. It is useful to the marketer as it often explores people's feelings and opinions.

Quantitative research – information that can be measured in numeric terms and analysed statistically.

Reference group – a group with which the customer identifies in some way and whose opinions and experiences influence the customer's behaviour.

Relationship marketing – the strategy of establishing a relationship with a customer which continues well beyond the first purchase.

Return on investment – the value that an organisation derives from investing in a project.

Sales promotion – a range of techniques used to increase sales in the short term.

Skimming – setting the original price high in the early stages of the product life cycle to get as much profit as possible before prices are driven down by increasing competition.

SLEPT – a framework for viewing the macro environment – Socio-cultural, Legal, Economic, Political and Technical factors.

SMART – a mnemonic referring to the need for objectives to be Specific, Measurable, Achievable, Relevant and Timebound.

Sponsorship – specialised form of promotion where a company will help fund an event or support a business venture in return for publicity.

Stakeholder – an individual or group that affects or is affected by the organisation and its operations.

Supplier – an organisation or individual that supplies goods or services to a company.

Targeting – the use of market segmentation to select and address a key group of potential purchasers.

Unique Selling Proposition (USP) – the benefit that a product or service can deliver to customers that is not offered by any competitor.

Vision – the long-term aims and aspirations of the company for itself.

Word-of-mouth – the spreading of information through human interaction alone.

Appendix 1

Feedback to Case Studies

Session 1 – The weakest link?

1. What are the implications of confusion marketing for organisations that are marketing oriented?

   - Risk of sending conflicting messages, as this is not consistent with putting the customer first. Customers and consumers like clear and concise messages that are easy to understand in order to help them make well-informed decisions.

   - Customers may not get the product that best meets their needs, so will not return and may tell others.

   - If they find products or services information too complex, they may not be motivated to purchase, preferring 'simpler' rival products.

   - Adverse publicity as mentioned in the Case Study.

2. How can organisations assess if they are treating their customers 'fairly' at the point of sale?

   - Monitor customer feedback.

   - Gather information from front-line staff on issues that cause confusion.

   - Carry out customer satisfaction surveys.

3. What else could companies like Virgin, who offer financial services, do to avoid confusion marketing?

   - Pilot new products to determine what issues might confuse.

   - Contact customers to find out what issues cause common confusion and make these the subject of a 'Frequently Asked Questions' (FAQs) on printed material and web site – i.e. be proactive rather than simply making it easier for customers to get help.

   - Use technology to set up systems that update customers on changing options in simple, jargon-free language.

   - Provide human support – face to face contact is still preferred by many customers.

Session 2 – E-volution in relationships

1. Communicating via email was seen as a major benefit for international customers. What are some of the uses that organisations might make of email to communicate with international customers and clients?

    ■ General communications on routine queries and progress reports.

    ■ Sending out invitations and paperwork for international conferences.

    ■ Sending large documents for approval.

2. What are the skills that might be lost if the use of email among staff rises at the expense of personal contact?

    ■ Questioning and listening skills.

    ■ Assertiveness.

    ■ Observation – responding to non-verbal communication.

    ■ Problem solving and decision making, because it is more difficult to brainstorm and build on each other's ideas.

    ■ Conflict resolution, because disagreements might not emerge.

    ■ Creativity.

    ■ Dealing with people face to face helps develop strong working relationships because generally people feel more commitment to the other person.

3. What are the potential disadvantages for organisations of using email to communicate with customers?

    ■ It is more difficult to deal with complex enquiries or those that are not routine.

    ■ Customers often like personal contact in the same way that they feel reassured by examining products in a shop before purchase, rather than shopping on the Internet.

    ■ There is no warmth or smile in an email communication!

Session 3 – Centrica

1. How has information been used to improve services at Centrica?

   - Individual complaints have been investigated.

   - Top reasons have been identified to help prioritise action.

   - Top and bottom of the company share real information so problems are identified as quickly as possible and the right people are involved in the solution.

2. What other information would be help Simon Waugh and Centrica develop a competitive edge on customer service?

   - Competitor's methods of handling complaints.

   - Competitor's service standards and compliance.

   - Customer perception of recent improvements at Centrica – if good, could be used in customer communications.

   - Suggestions from the sharp end about what customers feel is really important – what is most important to them.

3. What are the potential benefits for working relationships of Centrica's policy of encouraging senior managers to spend time in the field on a regular basis?

   - Each understands the other's viewpoints and problems so both find it easier to work towards a common goal.

   - Front-line staff should feel more valued, more ready to communicate openly – say what needs to be said.

   - Greater mutual respect and trust.

Session 4 – Net benefits

1. Why do lifestyle sites represent an ideal route to the student market?

   - Good penetration of the target market.

   - Wide acceptance of the medium.

   - Opportunity for soft-sell approach.

2. How can information on customer preferences be collected via the Internet?

    ■ Feedback forms.

    ■ Competitions.

    ■ Response buttons.

3. What are the lessons that other site owners can learn from hot-toast.com's approach to site design and content?

    ■ Designing content that appeals to target groups.

    ■ Use content providers that have wide acceptance by target groups.

    ■ Uncluttered homepage.

    ■ Avoid the hard-sell approach.

Session 5 – The great debate

1. The article highlights the collaborative approach taken by the people involved in designing the conference programme and content. How important do you think it is that event organisers also work closely with these people?

    ■ The event has very specific requirements in terms of facilities for group work, so it is critical that these are understood by event organisation staff.

    ■ The high level of interactivity means that delegate movements need to be carefully planned, so it is very important that any constraints on this are understood by the designers. It may be due to venue or health and safety if large numbers of people are moving from group to group and perhaps different areas of the venue.

    ■ Long-term relationships are developed by people working closely together to understand each other's needs.

2. What difficulties might planners encounter when planning such a 'different' event?

    ■ Planners might not be quite sure about facilities etc. required if they are departing from their usual conference structure, so may not give a good brief to organisers.

    ■ If trying out new ideas they might want to make changes to the programme – and therefore requirements – at short notice.

- The group-based nature of the conference programme might add to the cost significantly if additional syndicate rooms are required and some venues might not be able to accommodate large numbers of small groups in adjacent rooms, so conference delegates are spread over a large area. This might make co-ordination of delegate movement difficult.

3. What suggestions might you make regarding the venue to support the nature of the event to enhance success?

- As a creative event you might suggest a creative venue.

- Other creativity enhancers might include selecting a venue with a full range of relaxation and leisure facilities to enable delegates to refresh their minds and bodies!

- You may wish to suggest a venue with some outdoor facilities to get plenty of oxygen to delegates' brains!

Session 6 – New dimensions

1. Why are live events a good way to communicate brand image?

- They allow consumers to 'experience' the brand via different sensory experiences.

- Live events aid retention.

- They add an additional dimension in exciting emotions and senses.

2. If creating such an event, how important do you think it is to work closely with the brand manager and his/her team?

- Live events 'bring the brand to life' so it is important to understand the different elements that make up the brand.

- The experience has to appeal to consumers so organisers need to understand their characteristics.

- Organisers need to be aware of what the brand manager wants to achieve.

3. What might be the downside for Hotpoint of concluding the tour in a café overlooking the Millennium Dome?

- The Millennium Dome received negative media attention which might 'rub off' on the Hotpoint brand.

- The Millennium Dome was a temporary exhibition.

- Such a dominant attraction as the Millennium Dome might overpower the Hotpoint brand.

Session 7 – The international conference venue

1. You have been given a media budget of £55,000 and asked to produce a media plan for the next 6 months. It is now August. Justify your plan.

There are no right and wrong answers but you will need to be able to produce a reasoned argument for your plan.

Publication	Sep	Oct	Nov	Dec	Jan	Feb	No of inserts	Cost per insert	Total cost
The Conferencer	Double page	Page			Double pager	Page	4	£4,000 per page	£24,000
Venue Selector					Page		1	£10,000 per page	£10,000
Events & Exhibitions	Page	Page					2	£5,000 per page	£10,000
Sub-total									£44,000
Web redesign									£5,000
Web maintenance									£1,500
Advertising production									£5,500
Total									£56,000

In this case the marketer has gone for two main publications rather than spread the budget thinly between all publications:

- *The Conferencer* because it reaches decision makers, so used a double page and then page pattern of advertising, hoping that residual effects will last through November and December. If spring is the busy time then the earlier advertising should stimulate bookings for the next year.

- *The Venue Selector* because it is new and should attract interest – it also goes to opinion formers who influence other decision makers.

- *Events and Exhibitions* is a weekly so this could be tried out early on, perhaps with insertions 2 weeks apart. Caution here because it has a claimed readership, not authenticated circulation figures with reader profile.

- *Conference Management* – may be useful but senior executives may not be the decision makers, so not used initially.

Although the budget has been exceeded it may be possible to negotiate a discount of £1,000 or more with *The Conferencer* for booking a series of advertisements.

The marketer would also review where the opposition is advertising and take this into account when making a final decision.

2. What suggestions can you make to increase summer usage? What media would you use?

- Use this time to develop local trade through open days etc. advertised in the local press.

- Flyers in the local press or door to door offering off peak membership at reduced rates or three months' membership for families for the summer.

- Sponsor a local football team or project to get local publicity on radio, TV and newspapers.

- Mailshot local businesses offering discounted rates for multiple bookings or room hire.

3. What other media opportunities might you explore to raise awareness of IVC and its facilities?

- Advertising at the nearby international airport – posters, in-flight magazines etc.

- Articles/advertisements in local businesses newsletters.

Session 8 – Brave new ideas

1. What was the main benefit that Eyretel achieved by innovating the sales process?

By simplifying the process Eyretel has achieved:

- Reduction in expensive manpower going out to the customer.

- Reduction in administration because the expert system can cope with the order process and technical queries.

- Reputation for clarity and simplicity which often speeds up the time taken between enquiry and booked order.

2. Why do you think that sales representatives represent an effective way of reaching customers?

Sales representatives represent an effective way of reaching customers in many business to business markets because:

- Products are complex and require a skilled salesperson to help the customer understand how products meet requirements.

- Queries can be dealt with on the spot or quickly so the customer can make a fully informed choice without having to search for more information themselves.

3. What other channel of distribution might they use in the future?

- In the future customers may be able to purchase online if they are able to access a personal salesperson electronically who is able to deal with specific enquiries.

- Broadband application and digital technology may increase the speed of electronic communication and clarity, so good quality product demonstrations can be reproduced on the manufacturer's web sites, reducing the need for face to face demonstrations.

Session 9 – Giving is good business

1. What are the full range of benefits that the Royal & Sun Alliance Insurance Group expect to gain from community sponsorship?

- Local publicity that raises awareness among potential employees.

- To associate the brand with social responsibility.

- Enhance ethical reputation and image.

- Raise employee morale.

2. What might that the Royal & Sun Alliance Insurance Group do next to further communicate their sense of social responsibility?

    ▪ Communicate this through advertising.

    ▪ Develop news releases that emphasise activities and policies that are ethical, kind to the environment and promote their image as a caring company.

    ▪ Promote 'green' issues through energy efficiency and using recycled paper for printed materials.

3. Why is sponsorship a good way of promoting brand image?

    ▪ It creates an association in consumers' minds – which is why it is so important to select the sponsorship partner so carefully.

    ▪ It enables consumers to 'experience' the brand image.

    ▪ It provides evidence of brand image and publicity.

Session 10 – Centrica

1. How important do you think the P for People is for Centrica – what evidence can you read in the Case Study?

    ▪ Essential to success, hence the investment in training.

    ▪ Front-line staff are given high levels of support.

    ▪ The trial is a sign of Centrica's commitment to customer service.

2. How is Centrica preparing its people to provide high standards of service and why does this matter?

    ▪ Providing coaching, mentoring and counselling as individuals – looking after staff so they look after customers.

    ▪ It is unlikely that de-motivated staff will provide high levels of service.

    ▪ Investment in training – front-line staff need to have both knowledge of product and customer care skills to answer customer queries effectively and promptly.

    ▪ By focusing on the customer (internal and external), and meeting their needs, Centrica creates a culture of customer care which is important in service marketing if high standards are to be achieved.

3. What does the Case Study suggest are the difficulties for Centrica in the short term?

- Budget!

- The investment needs to be made upfront for benefits that will only be fully realised in the longer term.

- Justifying expenditure when short-term results are not predicted.

Session 11 – The Christmas catalogue – Wallbury's Plc

1. Draw up an estimate of the costs associated with producing a million copies of the catalogue, together with likely suppliers' contributions.

Cost of producing one million copies of catalogue:

Typesetting and preparation	100,000
Print costs (1,000 x £50)	50,000*
Photographs for 16 pages (3 x £50 x 32)	4,800**
Total estimate of costs	£154, 800

*£50 per thousand copies so costs £50,000 for one million.

**Assuming 6 photographs on each page including front and back cover. Half the photographs are available from suppliers, so base calculations on 3 per page not 6 per page.

NB: There are no costs noted for labour or overheads.

Suppliers' contributions:

- Revenue from advertising sales   £75,000***

***£15,000 from front and back cover plus 30 x £2,000 for remaining pages.

NB: Suppliers are also making a contribution of £4,800 by supplying the photographs. If this was not the case Wallbury's would incur this cost.

2. If it appears likely that the revenue for advertising sales on inside pages will be significantly reduced, what suggestions can you make for reducing costs?

- Reducing the number of pages in the catalogue.

- Reducing the number of photographs used or increasing the number contributed by suppliers.

- Negotiating with the printer to reduce print costs.

3. Wallbury's are considering producing a full online catalogue and prior to selling selected products online. What might their first actions be before setting a budget for this?

- Gathering information from customers on their potential usage of an online catalogue.

- Reviewing competitor's approach to e-marketing.

- Getting estimates of the costs involved and return on investment.

- Gathering information from suppliers on their willingness to purchase web advertising space and other possible contributions.

Session 12 – Property exhibitions

1. Due to budget cutbacks it has been decided that the company can only afford to attend one of the two exhibitions mentioned in the memo. Identify costings for each event.

Assumption: $1.50 = £1.00.

	Europrop (3 days)	Chicago industrial RE fair (4 days)
Stand space	£19,800 (3 x £6,600) 50 square metres	£16,000 (4 x £4,000) 40 square yards £24,000 60 square yards
Stand design	£6,000	£3,000
Staff	£2,400 (3 x 4 x £200)	£3,200 (4 x 4 x £200)

	Europrop (3 days)	Chicago industrial RE fair (4 days)
Travel	£800 (4 x £200)	£1,200 (4 x 300)
Expenses*	£2,700	£2,700

*Expenses for the longer event are similar due to the cheaper prices available in Chicago.

Costs for stand equipment and printed materials (brochures etc.) are similar.

2. Make a recommendation for attending one of the events and justify.

A case can be made for attending either event.

The company has a history of success at Europrop so the show organisers have proved that they can attract the right type of visitors for Tattersfield Property Holdings plc (TPH plc) and have promised that there will be 25% more. In addition, invitations can be sent to major customers who visited last year.

The Chicago Fair is a new event so visitor numbers are not proven. Although it offers an opportunity to reach a new audience it is a risk. If costs need to be cut then it is probably a wiser decision to attend the exhibition that has produced results in the past and use information about the previous show to make improvements on attracting visitors to the stand and interacting with visitors. As a shorter event, staff will be fresher on the final day and more alert to opportunities. The longer event may require more staff and has a higher overall cost.

3. What additional information would be useful to help make a final decision about which exhibition to attend?

- Event aims and objectives – what does TPH plc want to achieve?
- Visitor numbers and profiles (Europrop only).
- List of companies that exhibited last year (Europrop only).
- Projected visitor numbers and profiles.
- Evaluation report on Europrop last year.

- Detailed costings of stand equipment.
- Dates of shows to see how each fits with other marketing activities.
- Competitor activities.
- Budget for event and flexibility.

Appendix 2

Syllabus

Marketing in practice

Aim

The Marketing in Practice module is the application of marketing in context at Stage 1 and also forms the summative assessment for Stage 1. It aims to assist participants to integrate and apply knowledge from all the modules at Stage 1.

Participants will not be expected to have any prior qualifications or experience in a marketing role. They will be expected to be conversant with the content of the other 3 modules at Stage 1 before undertaking this module.

Related statements of practice

Hb.1 Contribute to project planning and budget preparation.

Hb.2 Monitor and report on project activities.

Hb.3 Complete and close down project activities on time and within budget.

Jb.1 Collect, synthesise, analyse and report measurement data.

Jb.2 Participate in reviews of marketing activities using measurement data.

Kb.1 Exchange information to solve problems and make decisions.

Kb.2 Review and develop one's skills and competencies.

Kb.3 Embrace change and modify behaviours and attitudes.

Learning outcomes

Participants will be able to:

- Collect relevant data from a variety of secondary information sources.

- Analyse and interpret written, visual and graphical data.

- Devise appropriate visual and graphical means to present marketing data.

- Make recommendations based on information obtained from multiple sources.

- Evaluate and select media and promotional activities appropriate to the organisation's objectives and status and to its marketing context.

- Calculate and justify budgets for marketing mix decisions.

- Develop relationships inside and outside the organisation.

- Apply planning techniques to a range of marketing tasks and activities.

- Undertake basic marketing activities within an agreed plan and monitor and report on progress.

- Gather information for, and evaluate marketing results against, financial and other criteria.

Knowledge and skill requirements

Element 1: Gathering, analysing and presenting information (20%) (Marketing Environment).

1.1 Identify sources of information internally and externally to the organisation, including ICT-based sources such as Intranet and Internet.

1.2 Maintain a marketing database, information collection and usage.

1.3 Investigate customers via the database and develop bases for segmentation.

1.4 Explain information gathering techniques available.

1.5 Source and present information on competitor activities across the marketing mix.

1.6 Investigate marketing and promotional opportunities using appropriate information gathering techniques.

1.7 Gather information across borders.

Element 2: Building and developing relationships (20%) (Customer Communications).

2.1 Describe the structure and roles of the marketing function within the organisation.

2.2 Build and develop relationships within the marketing department, working effectively with others.

2.3 Explain the 'front-line' role: receiving and assisting visitors, internal and external enquiries.

2.4 Represent the organisation using practical PR skills.

2.5 Explain the supplier interface: negotiating, collaborating, operational and contractual aspects.

2.6 Explain how the organisation fits into a supply chain and works with distribution channels.

2.7 Use networking skills in the business world.

2.8 Explain the concept and application of E-relationships.

2.9 Describe techniques available to assist in managing your manager.

Element 3: Organising and undertaking marketing activities (20%) (Marketing Fundamentals).

3.1 Describe the scope of individuals' roles in marketing: meetings, conferences, exhibitions, outdoor shows, outlet launches, press conferences.

3.2 Identify alternative and innovative approaches to a variety of marketing arenas and explain criteria for meeting business objectives.

3.3 Demonstrate an awareness of successful applications of marketing across a variety of sectors and sizes of business.

3.4 Explain how marketing makes use of planning techniques: objective setting; and co-ordinating, measuring and evaluating results to support the organisation.

3.5 Appraise and select a venue based on given criteria and make appropriate recommendations.

3.6 Explain how an organisation should host visitors from other cultures and organising across national boundaries.

Element 4: Co-ordinating the marketing mix (20%) (Marketing Fundamentals).

4.1 Select media to be used based on appropriate criteria for assessing media opportunities, and recommend a media schedule.

4.2 Evaluate promotional activities and opportunities including sales promotion, PR and collaborative programmes.

4.3 Explain the process for designing, developing and producing printed matter, including leaflets, brochures and catalogues.

4.4 Analyse the impact of pricing decisions and role of price within the marketing mix.

4.5 Describe the current distribution channels for an organisation and evaluate new opportunities.

4.6 Describe how organisations monitor product trends.

4.7 Explain the importance of the extended marketing mix: how process, physical aspects and people affect customer choice.

4.8 Explain the importance of ICT in the new mix.

Element 5: Administering the marketing budget (and evaluating results) (20%).

5.1 Demonstrate an ability to manipulate numbers in a marketing context.

5.2 Explain the process used for setting a budget and apportioning fixed and overhead costs.

5.3 Explain how organisations assess the viability of opportunities, marketing initiatives and projects.

5.4 Prepare, present and justify a budget as the basis for a decision on a marketing promotion.

5.5 Make recommendations on alternative courses of action.

5.6 Examine the correlation between marketing mix decisions and results.

5.7 Evaluate the cost effectiveness of a marketing budget, including a review of suppliers and activities.

Appendix 3

Specimen examination paper

The Chartered
Institute of Marketing

Certificate in Marketing

Marketing in Practice

5.26:   **Marketing in Practice**

Time:

Date:

3 Hours Duration

This examination is in two sections.

PART A – Is compulsory and worth 40% of total marks.

PART B – Has **SIX** questions; select **THREE**. Each answer will be worth 20% of the total marks.

DO NOT repeat the question in your answer, but show clearly the number of the question attempted on the appropriate pages of the answer book.

Rough workings should be included in the answer book and ruled through after use.

© The Chartered Institute of Marketing

Certificate in Marketing

5.26:   Marketing in Practice – Specimen Paper

PART A

bizinfo/hungary.com

Following the collapse of Communism, the markets of Central and Eastern Europe have undergone massive change, and there is a great deal of inward investment by American, British and Multinational companies.

bizinfo/hungary.com was established three years ago by a former real estate salesman and an IT specialist. It serves as an English language portal (an Internet gateway) for a range of services needed by incoming investors, and provides comprehensive listings and information on property and land for commercial and residential use. There is also a subscription service for more detailed financial and business news, not just from Hungary, but also from the Czech and Slovak Republics and Romania.

Only six people are employed full-time by the company and the biggest expenditure is on advertising in order to ensure the maximum number of 'hits' on the web site. Advertising is placed not just in Hungary, but also in business publications in Western Europe, Asia Pacific and the USA.

The company has been successful and a similar operation is now planned for Turkey, which is looking towards European Union membership. The launch of bizinfo/turkey.com is only three months away and nothing has yet been done to publicise it in Istanbul. Looking further ahead, Estonia is also under consideration as it could serve not only the Baltic States but also Poland.

Your Role

You have just arrived in your exciting new job as the company's first Marketing Assistant, and have soon realised what a fast moving business environment this is. The Financial Controller is calling for reductions in expenditure, your relationship with the current advertising agency is unsettled, yet meanwhile, the company is about to expand rapidly. Also, bizinfo has little idea of who is actually visiting its web site, and there is an urgent need to gather information on site visitors via an electronic questionnaire.

Strictly Confidential

To: A. Jeffrey

In view of the planned expansion into two new countries, we need to carefully control our costs and **we need to make a 10% saving on all our expenditure including advertising**. This could possibly be achieved by moving away from our current Full Service Agency when its contract expires next month. We could then buy media and creative work from whoever offers the cheapest prices.

Attached are some figures obtained from our current agency and also quotes from a media buyer and a newly established creative agency.

Also, to help you understand how the business works I have enclosed a summary of costings and revenues from each of our three activities.

I trust this will be useful.

F. Varos
Financial Controller

Advertising Costs

Current Situation

bizinfo/hungary.com has an annual contract with Eurinter Advertising plc., who charges a monthly fee of $1,000 to cover account management and the production of visuals. Production costs for each of the four advertising campaigns in a typical year work out at an average of $3,000 each. The 10% average discount obtained on media expenditure means we spend $900,000 on media costs.

Alternatively...

Medialink Media Buying Company are confident of obtaining an average discount of 12% across the publications and media we currently use. Hotshots Creative charges $500 for visuals or roughs of proposed advertising and has quoted $5,000 for production of finished advertisements for a campaign.

The Company's Activities

bizinfo/hungary.com/businessportal

This service gives links to a full range of business services needed by incoming investors; translation services, legal services, investment advisors, software designers etc. etc. The service is free but advertising on banners and around the portal generates $350,000 per year.

bizinfo/hungary.com/property

This service is again free to site visitors but generates revenue from property developers and real estate agencies whose properties are featured on the web site. This has many search features to save the time of those looking to set up in Hungary or base their staff in the country. This generates $800,000 per year.

bizinfo/hungary.com/businessnews

This subscription-only service has 1,500 subscribers paying $10 per month for the latest financial and investment news.

The Company's Costs

An advertising sales manager, whose wage is $20,000 per year, manages the two free services, whilst a journalist is employed on the same wage to run the news service. Other costs, including wages, technical support and office rental amount to $180,000 per year. (This is divided between the three services.) There is also the cost of advertising as detailed earlier.

PART A

Question 1.

a.   Will a move to separate buying of creative work and media give the required 10% saving on advertising costs over a twelve month period? (Show your calculations and state any assumptions you have made).

(15 marks)

b.   What should be contained in a brief for an advertising agency? Provide a sample briefing document containing the information that is needed.

(15 marks)

c.   What problems are likely to arise when dealing with a new supplier and how are these best avoided?

(10 marks)
(40 marks in total)

PART B – Answer THREE Questions Only

Question 2.

As part of a marketing audit being undertaken by bizinfo.com you have been asked to investigate the competition. As part of this process:

a.   How will you identify competitors?

(7 marks)

b.   What information do you need?

(6 marks)

c.   How will you obtain and verify the information?

(7 marks)
(20 marks in total)

Question 3.

A launch event is planned for 100 guests from local businesses and the media in Istanbul.

a.   What steps need be taken to ensure the smooth running of the event?

(10 marks)

b.   Produce a Gantt chart showing tasks needing to be undertaken before and after the event takes place in three months' time.

(10 marks)
(20 marks in total)

Question 4.

How can all the elements of the promotional submix be used to promote bizinfo, a virtual company?

(20 marks)

Question 5.

Which is currently the most profitable of the company's three areas of business and how would this change if the savings were implemented? Justify your answer with appropriate calculations.

(20 marks)

Question 6.

a. Draft a letter to potential advertisers on your web site in Hungary, selling the company's offering.

(10 marks)

b. Suggest ways other than mailing by which businesses can be approached, highlighting the advantages and disadvantages of such methods.

(10 marks)
(20 marks in total)

Question 7.

What information does bizinfo need about the visitors to its web site, and how can this be used to further build the business?

(20 marks)

Appendix 4

Feedback to specimen exam paper

The following do not represent full answers to the Specimen Examination Paper, but look at:

- The rationale for the question – what the Examiner is looking for.
- The best way to structure your answer.
- The key points that you should have included and expanded upon.
- How marks for the question might have been allocated.
- The main syllabus area that is being assessed.

Part A

Question 1.

1a.

Cost analysis of current situation (full service)

12 x $1,000 fees	=	12,000
4 x $3,000 ad campaigns	=	12,000
Media costs (inc.10% discount)	=	900,000 (100,000 less 10% discount)
Total	=	$924,000

Cost analysis of alternative situation (creative work + media buying separate)

Media costs	=	880,000 (100,000 less 12% discount)
Creative work + production 4 x $5,500	=	22,000
Total	=	$902,000

Cost comparison:

Full service	=	$924,000
Separate services	=	$902,000
Potential saving	=	$22,000 (2.4%) which does not meet the target of 10%

Assumptions:

- The company buys the same amount of media space over the next year.
- The company runs four campaigns over the next year.
- The price of advertising space remains the same.

1b.

Organisation:	
Department:	Date: Prepared by:
Campaign objectives:	
Product details including features, benefits and USP:	
Target audience:	
Message to be communicated:	
Budget:	
Timescale:	
Corporate literature attached: ■ Company handbook giving details of vision and values. ■ Examples of previous campaigns. ■ Corporate literature to illustrate logo positioning and corporate colours.	
Contact details:	
Signed for the company:	Signed for the Agency:

1c.

Potential problems:

■ Agency may not fully understand the client organisation's vision, values and how to communicate these – this may delay progress.

- Client is unlikely to commit to a long-term relationship until the first few campaigns have proved successful, so the Agency will feel as if it is 'on trial' so interpersonal relationships may not be easy.

- Each party will not be used to each others' way of working which could lead to misunderstandings.

- The contacts from each side have not got to know each other so meetings may be very formal and more time consuming, as every point is discussed in detail to check each other's understanding.

Avoiding problems:

- Select new agency carefully, taking up references and setting the agency a test project – provide full brief and information about the organisation so the Agency can get a 'feel' for their client.

- Take time to build good working relationships and get to know each other by meeting face to face, stating clearly what is required, being firm but fair and consistent, listening to the Agency and making them feel part of the team, putting requirements in writing and setting realistic deadlines.

- Make sure that the Agency are aware of the nature of the relationship – will this be a long-term relationship if they meet expectations or is it a short-term contract only?

- Make sure that the Agency understand how to meet needs and what the consequences are if these are not met – provide accurate and full written briefings.

Question 2.

2a.

To identify competitors providing similar services contact reliable information sources internal and external to bizinfo/hungary.com.

Internal sources:

- Company staff.
- Previous marketing audits.
- Existing market reports and records.

External sources:

- Commercial publications listing enterprises working in central and eastern Europe.

- Market reports.

- Investment trade press.

- Business press.

- Hungarian agencies supporting inward investment and development.

- Internet.

- Customers.

- Chamber of Commerce and Industry.

2b.

Information on competitors:

- Who they are and which market sectors they target.

- Market share, size of company.

- Reputation and when they were established.

- Nature of services provided.

- Main customers.

- Promotional activity.

- Business aims and objectives – current and future.

2c.

Information can be obtained from:

- Secondary sources listed above and primary research (interview – may be face to face or telephone) among staff and customers.

- Secondary sources of information, such as business directories, are available at libraries and Chamber of Commerce and market information is available from investment trade association and government web sites – site addresses can be found by using appropriate search engines.

- Chamber of Commerce and Industry carry directories of suppliers listed by market sector – they can be contacted by telephone.

- Reading the investment trade press will identify main competitors.

The easiest way to check the validity of information is to visit competitor web sites, view details of services and request further information.

Also check that secondary sources used are up to date and check for possible bias.

Cross reference information from different sources to check validity.

Question 3.

3a.

To ensure the smooth running of the event:

- Check that SMART objectives have been set and that a sound project plan is in place.
- Identify who should be invited and send invitations promptly – these should be personalised.
- Select an appropriate venue – see checklist in Session 5.
- Employ local staff to host so they will be culturally acclimatised.
- Brief staff on the event objectives and the contribution to achievement each must make.
- Ensure a good ratio of hosting staff to guests so guests are well looked after from the moment they arrive to the time they leave.
- Produce a clear and concise press pack.

3b.

Gantt chart

	Month One		Month Two		Month Three		*After the event
Select project team							
Set event objectives							
Decide who to invite							
Select and book venue							

	Month One		Month Two		Month Three		*After the event
Decide event programme		▓					
Send invitations with RSVP (press and guests)			▓				
Check speakers' needs			▓				
Check equipment needed			▓				
Brief staff – assess training needs		▓					
Carry out staff training				▓	▓		
Check number attending – use reserve list if few positive replies				▓			
Prepare press pack					▓		
Organise printed materials					▓		
Final briefing for staff						▓	
Final briefing for venue						▓	
Send out news release						▓	
Debrief with staff							▓
Debrief with project team							▓
Develop database of contacts							▓
Send out letter to those attending							▓
Monitor press and other media coverage							▓
Evaluate event against objectives							▓

*Debriefing should take place as soon as possible after the event.
Follow-up letters should go out immediately (prepared in advance).
Other activities should begin immediately and are ongoing.

Question 4.

Identify the elements of the promotional submix – advertising, sales promotion, personal selling, PR, sponsorship, personal selling and direct mail. Begin with a short paragraph on the need to co-ordinate promotional activities to create synergy and ensure consistency of communication. Also identify the need to set promotional objectives and identify how each element contributes to achievement of these objectives.

Structure your answer under headings – elements of the submix.

Remember to contextualise your answer – you are promoting a virtual company.

Be realistic and specific – for example, do not just state that an appropriate PR activities could be implemented, but identify what, how and why.

Review your answer against the above checklist.

Question 5.

Calculations to show the most profitable area of bizinfo/hungary.com:

	Businessportal	Property	Businessnews
Revenue	350,000	800,000	150,000
Variable costs			
Ad production	(4,000)	(4,000)	(4,000)
Media costs	(300,000)	(300,000)	(300,000)
Contribution	46,000	496,000	(154,000)
Fixed costs			
Ad sales manager	(10,000)	(10,000)	
Journalist			(20,000)
Overheads	(60,000)	(60,000)	(60,000)
Ad monthly fee (A/C mgt.)	(4,000)	(4,000)	(4,000)
Profit/Loss	**(28,000)**	**422,000**	**(238,000)**

The property section is the most profitable area of the business. Reducing expenditure by 10% would not alter this result.

Note that expenditure is shared equally across the three sections – the main difference is the cost of labour.

Question 6.

6a.

Use business letter format on corporate headed stationery.

Corporate address and logo

Date

Contact Name
Company address

Dear Mr XXXXXXX

Web Advertising – Lower rates for the next 3 months

Further to our telephone conversation on XXXXXX, I am writing to introduce bizinfo/hungary.com and the advertising opportunities that we can offer your company.

As a successful and forward looking organisation, we provide a wide range of services to inward investors including comprehensive listings and information on property and land for commercial and residential use. We currently deal with over 2,000 enquiries a week through our web site, many of whom have been recommended by previous clients.

Bizinfo/hungary.com is now planning to launch its services in a number of new locations, including Turkey in three months' time. Consequently, we are now able to offer companies such as yourselves the opportunity to advertise on our web site at a very competitive rate which is around 10% less than normal charges. This is available for all advertisements booked in the next three months.

Feedback from our existing advertisers illustrates the benefits that our customers experience:

List two testimonials.

Further benefits for yourselves include:

List benefits such as credit terms for payment, opportunities to reach wide range of markets etc.

I would be delighted to discuss the above with you further and will call you next week to see if you are interested in taking up our offer now or in the near future.

Yours sincerely

6b.

Other methods of approaching businesses include:

Telemarketing – cold calling is quick method of obtaining a response but unsolicited calls are not always welcome. For best results find out who to contact and make an appointment to phone them at a time that is convenient for them. Those that are not interested will not make an appointment.

Personal contact – face to face selling is labour intensive and costly. However, a good salesperson can develop a positive working relationship with potential customers and enhance loyalty.

Email – similar to direct mail. Inexpensive but needs to be accurately targeted to achieve a good response. Unsolicited emails may not be opened or binned.

Advertising – as mentioned in the Case Study.

Exhibitions – costly but useful if important decision makers attend.

Question 7.

Information needed includes:

- Who are they?
- How many?
- What do they want/need?
- Where do they come from?
- Why are they visiting?
- When do they visit?
- How many times do they visit?
- What do they think of us?
- When did they last buy from us or rivals?

The information can be used to:

- Develop a contact database for future promotions.
- Identify market segments.
- Improve services to meet current and future needs.
- Measure effectiveness of services.
- Determine competitive edge.
- Attract new customers.
- Attract repeat business.

Appendix 5

Assessment guidance

There are two methods used for assessment of candidates – Examination <u>or</u> Continuous Assessment via project.

The Chartered Institute of Marketing has traditionally used professional, externally set examinations as the means of assessment for the Certificate, Advanced Certificate and Postgraduate Diploma in Marketing. In 1995, at the request of industry, students and tutors, it introduced a continuously assessed route to two modules, one at Certificate level, and one at Advanced Certificate. With the increased emphasis on marketing practice, all modules are now open to assessment through Examination or Assessed Project.

The information in this appendix will:

- Help you prepare for Continuous Assessment.

- Provide hints and tips to help you prepare for the Examination.

- Manage your time effectively in preparing for Assessment.

NB: Your tutor will inform you which method of assessment applies to your programme.

Preparing for continuous assessment

If being assessed by Project you will be given a full brief for the assignment which will include what you have to do, how it is to be presented and the weighting of marks for each section. **You must read this before you start and check your understanding with your tutor.**

The assignment will consist of a number of tasks with weighting, so make sure you take account of this in your final presentation of the project.

The size of the project will be identified by a recommended word count. Check your final word count carefully but remember that quality is more important than quantity.

The Assignment tasks will include a reflective statement. This requires you to identify what you have learned from the experience of undertaking the module and how you have applied that learning in your job.

Questions you might want to consider to help you write this reflective statement include: What was the most difficult part? How did you feel at the start of the exercise and how do you feel at the end? Did you achieve your objectives? If not, why not? What have you learned about yourself as you have worked through the module? How much of your learning have you been able to apply at work? Have you been able to solve any real work problems through work you have done in your Assignments?

This statement will be personal to you, and should look forward to points you have identified as needing work in the future. We never stop learning – keep up this process of Continuous Professional Development as you go through your studies and you will have acquired the habit by the time you need to employ it to achieve Chartered Marketer status!

Examinations

Each subject differs slightly from the others, and style of question will differ between module examinations. All are closed book examinations apart from Analysis and Decision (see below).

For all examinations, apart from Marketing in Practice (see below), the examination paper consists of two sections:

Part A – Mini-case, scenario or article.

This section has a mini-case, scenario or article with compulsory questions. You are required to make marketing or sales decisions based on the information provided. You will gain credit for the decisions and recommendations you make on the basis of the analysis itself. This is a compulsory section of the paper designed to evaluate practical marketing skills.

Part B – Examination questions.

You will have a choice from a number of questions; when answering, ensure that you understand the context of those that you select. Rough plans for each answer are recommended.

The examination for Marketing in Practice differs in that the compulsory questions and examination questions are all linked to the mini-case and additional relevant information given, such as memos and reports.

The examination for Analysis and Decision is an open book examination and in the form of a Case Study. This is mailed out 4 weeks before the examination and posted on the CIM web site at the same time. Analysis and preparation should be completed during these four weeks. The questions asked in the examination will require strategic marketing decisions and actions. The question paper will also include additional unseen information about the Case Study.

CIM code of conduct for examinations

If being assessed by this method you will receive examination entry details which include a leaflet entitled 'Rules for Examinations'. Read these carefully because you will be penalised by CIM if you are in breach of any of these.

Most are common sense. For example, for closed book examinations you are not allowed to take notes or scrap paper into the examination room and must use the examination paper supplied to make rough notes and plans for your answer.

If you are taking the Analysis and Decision examination ensure that you **do** take your notes in with you, together with a copy of the Case Study.

Hints and tips

There are a number of places that you will be able to access information to help you prepare for your examination if you are being assessed by this method. Your tutor will give you good advice, and exam hints and tips can also be found on the CIM web site.

Some fundamental points are listed below:

- Read the question carefully and think about what is being asked before tackling the answer. The examiners are looking for knowledge, application and context. Refer back to the question to help you put your answer in the appropriate context. Do not just regurgitate theory.

- Consider the presentation style of your answer. For example, if asked to write a report then use report format with number headings – not essay style.

- Structure – plan your answer to make it easy for the examiner to see the main points that you are making.

- Timing – spread your time in proportion to the marks allocated and ensure that all required questions are answered.

- Relevant examples – the examiners expect relevant theory to be illustrated by practical examples. These can be drawn from your own experience, reading of current journals and newspapers or observations. Visit 'Hot Topics' on the CIM web site to see discussion of topical marketing issues and practice.

Managing your time

What is effective time management?

It's using wisely one of your most precious resources – TIME – to achieve your key goals. You need to be aware of how you spend your time each day, and set priorities so you know what's important to you, and what isn't. You need to establish goals for your study, work and family life and plan how to meet those goals. Through developing these habits you will be better able to achieve the things that are important to you.

When study becomes one of your key goals you may find that, temporarily, something has to be sacrificed in favour of time needed for reading, writing notes, writing up Assignments, preparing for group assessment, etc. It will help to 'get people on your side'. Tell people that you are studying and ask for their support – these include direct family, close friends and colleagues at work.

Time can just slip through your fingers if you don't manage it – and that's wasteful! When you are trying to balance the needs of family, social life, working life and study there is a temptation to leave Assignments until the deadline is near. Don't give in to this temptation! Many students have been heard to complain about the heavy workload towards the end of the course, when, in fact, they have had several months to work on Assignments; they have created this heavy workload themselves.

By knowing how to manage your time wisely you can:

- Reduce pressure when you're faced with deadlines or a heavy schedule.
- Be more in control of your life by making better decisions about how to use your time.
- Feel better about yourself because you're using your full potential to achieve.
- Have more energy for things you want or need to accomplish.
- Succeed more easily because you'll know what you want to do and what you need to do to achieve it.

Finally

Remember to continue to apply your new skills within your job – study and learning that is not applied is wasted time, effort and money! Well done and keep it up.

Index

See also the Glossary on page 227.

You may find referring back to the Learning Outcomes and the Summary of Key Points at the beginning and end of each Session will aid effective use of the Index.

Only where subjects are relevantly discussed or defined are they indexed.